FEMINISM AND POETRY

FEMINISM AND POETRY

LANGUAGE, EXPERIENCE, IDENTITY IN WOMEN'S WRITING

Jan Montefiore

London and New York

First published in 1987 by
Pandora Press (Routledge & Kegan Paul Ltd)
11 New Fetter Lane, London EC4P 4EE

Published in the USA by
Pandora Press (Routledge & Kegan Paul Inc.)
in association with Methuen Inc.
29 West 35th Street, New York, NY 10001

Set in 11/12 pt Sabon
by Columns of Reading
and printed in Great Britain
by the Guernsey Press Co Ltd,
Guernsey, Channel Islands

Library of Congress Cataloging in Publication Data

Montefiore, Jan.
Feminism and poetry.
Bibliography: p.
Includes index.
1. American poetry – Women authors – History and
criticism.   2. Feminism and literature – United States.
3. American poetry – 20th century – History and
criticism.   4. English Poetry – Women authors – History
and criticism.   5. Feminism and literature –
Great Britain.   6. English poetry – 20th century –
History and criticism.   I. Title.
PS310.F45M66   1987   811'.009'9287   86–30632

British Library CIP Data also available

ISBN 0–86358–162–5 (c)
ISBN 0–86358–163–3 (p)

CONTENTS

PREFACE AND ACKNOWLEDGMENTS

This book is about women's poetry and the ways in which feminist criticism reads and theorizes it. I am concerned throughout with two opposed but related topics: first, the question of what is specific to women's poetry, and second, the ways in which women poets engage with the masculine discourses by which poetry is normally defined, which at once do and don't include women. I begin with a discussion of women's experience in poetry; after that, the first part of the book is concerned with the subject of women in tradition; that is, both the ways in which women poets negotiate their own relation to English poetic tradition, and their creation of a tradition of their own. In the second half of the book I develop the subject of specifically female experience and language into a discussion of women's identity in poetry, drawing extensively on the concepts of identity developed by psychoanalysis, especially the work of Jacques Lacan on the concept of Imaginary identity and of Luce Irigaray on women's alienation in language. Much of this material is necessarily complex and difficult, but I have tried to avoid jargon and to make the arguments clear for the non-specialist reader.

Because this book is not a survey of women poets in general (or even of women poets writing in English in the mid-to-late twentieth century), but rather an attempt to theorize both the problems of women's poetry and some of the solutions, I have had to be selective in my choice of the poetry to be discussed in detail. Each chapter begins with a theoretical exposition, which is then worked through detailed criticism of the work of particular poets, who are mainly though not exclusively American and English women writing in the twentieth century, with Americans slightly predominating. I have consciously tried to focus on poems which have had little – and in some cases no – previous critical attention either from 'mainstream' or feminist criticism: many of the texts discussed may be new to readers. Women's poetry is much richer and more various than has been generally recognized: this book, though not a survey, does attempt to bring to readers' notice some of the unknown or unfamiliar work by women. For the same reason, I have devoted relatively little space to women poets whose work is already widely known, like Emily Dickinson and Sylvia Plath (though my extensive discussions of Adrienne Rich are obvious exceptions to this rule). All this selectivity has inevitably led to omissions which I regret. There are women poets whom I admire but whose work I have not mentioned (notably Elizabeth Bishop, Gwendolyn Brooks, Denise Levertov, Mina Loy and Marianne Moore) and others whom I discuss only briefly or in passing (such as Elizabeth Barrett Browning, Emily Dickinson, H.D., Charlotte Mew and Sylvia Plath). I am also aware that Black women poets, except for Audre Lorde, get little coverage. If I had had more time for research, this book would have been more inclusive. I hope, however, that one good result of these gaps will be to make clear that this book is intended to open debate, *not* to be an ideally comprehensive last word on women's poetry.

I am grateful to the Board of English and American Literature at the University of Kent for giving me a term's study leave in which to draft part of the book, and a year's leave of absence which has enabled me to edit and re-write the manuscript. Many people helped me during the writing of the book with conversation and ideas; I should particularly like to thank Claire Buck, John Ellis, Laura Marcus, and Michael Worton; also Sheila Shulman for courteously answering queries and directing me to the work of Irena Klepfisz. I am also grateful to the students of the Women's Studies MA at the University of Kent who attended the seminar on the 'Feminist Aesthetic', especially Roisin Battel, Iris Dove, Wilma Fraser and Val Heys, and also to Kate McLuskie, together with whom I taught this course; also the members of the Psycho-Analysis group at the University of Kent, especially Stephen Bann, Ben Brewster, Elizabeth Cowie and Martin Stanton, for shared ideas and feedback: also my editor, Philippa Brewster for her helpful directions, especially at the editing stage of the book. Finally I thank the many people who helped me out with child care, especially my sister Catherine Grace, and my husband Patrick Cockburn for his encouragement and support throughout the whole enterprise.

Portions of Chapters 1 and 2 first appeared as articles: 'In Her Own Image: Contemporary Women Poets', in *Poetry South-East* (Autumn 1981), and 'Feminist Identity and the Poetic Tradition', in *Feminist Review*, no. 13 (Spring 1983).

Although every attempt has been made to locate copyright holders, I have been unable to contact some of them, to whom I offer my apologies. I would like to thank the following for permission to reprint copyright material: Kingsley Amis for 8 lines from his poem 'A Bookshop Idyll', from *A Case of Samples*; Anvil Press Poetry Ltd for 3 lines from 'Christmas Sermon', from Peter Levi, *Collected Poems*; Georges Borchardt, Inc., for an extract from Monique Wittig, *The Lesbian Body*; the Literary Executors of Vera Brittain for 1 line from 'To

My Brother', from *Verses of a V.A.D.*, quoted from *Scars Upon My Heart*, ed. Catherine Reilly (Virago, 1981); Carcanet Press Ltd for 16 lines from 'Drawing you, heavy with sleep', from Sylvia Townsend Warner, *Collected Poems*, ed. Claire Harman (Carcanet, 1982); Carcanet Press Ltd and New Directions Publishing Corporation for 6 lines from 'Tribute to the Angels' and 4 lines from 'The Walls Do Not Fall', from H.D., *Trilogy* (Carcanet, 1973) (Copyright © 1973 by Norman Holmes Pearson); Faber & Faber Ltd and Harcourt Brace Jovanovich, Inc., for 2 lines from 'The Love Song of J. Alfred Prufrock', from T.S. Eliot, *Collected Poems 1909–1962*; Faber & Faber Ltd and Random House, Inc., for 10 lines from 'The Question', from W.H. Auden, *Collected Poems*, ed. Edward Mendelson (Copyright 1934 and renewed 1962 by W.H. Auden); Harvard University Press for poems 284, 518 and 640 from *The Poems of Emily Dickinson*, ed. Thomas H. Johnson (Copyright © 1951, 1955, 1979, 1983 by the President and Fellows of Harvard College); David Higham Associates Ltd for 'Easter Monday: in memoriam E.T.', from Eleanor Farjeon, *First and Second Love* (Oxford University Press, 1959); Houghton Mifflin Company and A.D. Peters & Co. Ltd for 11 lines from 'Snow White', 7 lines from 'Rumpelstiltskin', 3 lines from 'Briar Rose' and 21 lines from 'Rapunzel', from Anne Sexton, *Transformations* (Copyright © 1971 by Anne Sexton); Irena Klepfisz for extracts from *'Bashert'*, published in *Different Enclosures: Poetry and Prose of Irena Klepfisz* (Onlywomen Press, 1985) and in *Keeper of Accounts* (Sinister Wisdom Books, Montpelier, Vermont, 1983); Little, Brown and Company and Harvard University Press for 4 lines from poem 601 from *The Complete Poems of Emily Dickinson*, ed. Thomas H. Johnson (Copyright 1929 by Martha Dickinson Bianchi; Copyright © renewed 1957 by Mary L. Hampson); James MacGibbon, executor, for 8 lines from 'The Frog Prince', 14 lines from 'I rode with my darling' and 35 lines from

'Angel Boley', from Stevie Smith, *Collected Poems* (Penguin Modern Classics); Onlywomen Press and Alison Fell for 10 lines from 'Girl's Gifts', from *One Foot on the Mountain: An Anthology of British Feminist Poetry 1969–1979*, ed. Lilian Mohin (Onlywomen Press, 1979); Onlywomen Press and Sheila Shulman for 12 lines from 'Hard Words, or why lesbians have to be philosophers', from *One Foot on the Mountain*, ed. Lilian Mohin; Oxford University Press for 10 lines from Anne Stevenson, *Correspondences*, and 14 lines from 'Black Mountain, Green Mountain', from Anne Stevenson, *Minute by Minute*; Sidgwick & Jackson for 16 lines from Judith Kazantzis, *The Wicked Queen; Times Literary Supplement* for 3 lines from Carol Rumens, 'Outside Oswiecim'; Virago Press Ltd for 11 lines from 'Sing a Song of Wartime', from *Scars Upon My Heart*, ed. Catherine Reilly; A.P. Watt Ltd on behalf of the Executors of the Estate of Robert Graves for 1 line from 'To Juan at the Winter Solstice' and 2 lines from 'Dialogue on a Headland', from Robert Graves, *Poems Selected by Himself*; Yale University Press for 8 lines from 'Amazon Twins', 10 lines from 'Artemis' and 8 lines from 'Rapunzel', from Olga Broumas, *Beginning with O*.

CHAPTER 1

INTRODUCTORY: POETRY AND WOMEN'S EXPERIENCE

1 Poetry as experience: radical feminism

If this book does nothing else, it should make clear, first, that the range, scope and variety of women's poetry are thoroughly impressive, and second, that the question of women's 'difference' in poetry is an important and complex one. Defining a feminist poetics means, primarily, understanding the significance of women's poetry. This entails creating and defining the terms in which the poetry itself is to be understood, which also means taking a subject usually considered marginal as the centre not only of a study but also of an aesthetic: difficult exercises, both.

For to say that women's poems have only been granted a marginal status in poetry criticism is simply to state the obvious. As feminist scholars[1] have documented, women poets are frequently undervalued. If recognized, they are often misread – as with those studies of Emily Dickinson and Sylvia Plath[2] which read their poems for evidence of the poets's eccentricity and/or neurosis; or they get dismissed because women are supposed to have produced few or inadequate 'great poets' (an assertion now relatively seldom made in print,[3] but familiar in the classroom); or they are simply ignored – a phenomenon which I explore in some detail later in this chapter. More beguilingly, it is sometimes argued that women's poetry does not exist in a category by itself: there are simply good, bad and mediocre poems, whose writer's gender is as little relevant to their quality as her colour or class. This is a disingenuous or, at best, misleading argument, since these factors are exceedingly relevant to what is *considered* quality, or even legitimacy, by the journals, publishing houses, universities and schools through which poems are taught, judged, interpreted and published, largely dominated as these have been by people ignorant of and uninterested in women's poetry. What is important about such arguments is not their intellectual validity, which is slight, but their ideological defensiveness. They betray the fact that poetic tradition is itself an area of political and intellectual struggle.

On the other hand, the critical dismissal of women's poems has never been universal, or no woman poet would ever have been published, much less noticed. The overall situation for women's poetry has greatly improved over the last decade, thanks partly to the rise of women's publishing houses, feminist journals, and women's studies courses, and partly to feminist prodding within existing institutions. Yet the woman poet's marginal status remains in readers' perceptions: people feel, however unjustifiably, that the woman poet is a slight and freakish phenomenon compared with her substantial sister the novelist, let alone her massive and weighty poetic grand-fathers. And women poets have been much aware of the potential contradiction between their own marginal status as women and the high ambition implied in becoming a poet:

> I am obnoxious to each carping tongue
> That says, my hand a needle better fits[4]

Anne Bradstreet's apprehensions are still justified: the exclusion of women poets from the canon of tradition still persists, as emerges from the example of the critical history of the writing of the 1930s, discussed below pp. 20–5).

Over the past fifteen years, these traditional assumptions about the marginality of women's poetry have been challenged, especially in America, by radical feminist poets. As titles like Joan Larkin's *Housework* and Judy Grahn's 'Common Woman Poems' indicate, these poets put female experience at the centre of their aesthetic, which, since they have not been much interested in critical theory, one finds more often implied than articulated.[5] I would summarize such an aesthetic roughly as follows:

'Poetry is, primarily, the stuff of experience rendered into speech; a woman's poems are the authentic speech of her life and being.[6] In reading or listening to a woman's poem, we share the poet's experience, which is the experience of suffering and resistance common to all women, and we enter into her mind. Women's poetry is a huge resource of both female and feminist meaning, and it is crucial that we identify a tradition of specifically female poetry, not in order to "place" particular poems, but so as to understand female experiences (including sexual oppression), and woman's awareness and criticism of those experiences, as the intellectual and emotional context of the poetry we value.'[7]

An understanding of women's experience of oppression as central to our poetry has of course been influential among feminist critics: some assumptions like those outlined are discernable in the way Suzanne Juhasz's *Naked and Fiery Forms* (1976) emphasized the confessional element in women poets, or the way that some of the essays collected in *Shakespeare's Sisters* (ed. Sandra Gilbert and Susan Gubar, 1979) put their critical focus on the way poems exemplify their female creators' lives.[8] But, partly because my book deliberately deals with many poems which have had little or no attention from the comparatively small existing body of feminist criticism, and partly because these arguments and assumptions appear with most vitality, clarity and subtlety in the work of poets, I have taken these, rather than professional critics, as the representatives of radical feminist poetry criticism, directing my arguments mainly at poems and manifestos. It seems to me that – simply because of the ambitious poet's necessary struggle with language, form and reality – the most interesting thinking about the possibilities of radical feminist poetry has been done in the poems themselves, not in discursive or descriptive prose: even Adrienne Rich is far more subtle in her poems than in her essays.

Though I greatly respect radical feminism as a powerful, persuasive and consistent basis for poetry criticism, I have many disagreements with its assumptions as I understand them, in spite of the good influence they have exerted. Like all readers of women's poetry, I am politically and intellectually indebted to the work of radical feminists, particularly Adrienne Rich, who have not only resurrected unknown or undervalued poets[9] but have helped so to change the terms of critical debate that it is now easy to see women's poetry as valuable and important in itself. And since the radical feminist disregard for traditional literary criticism as uncomprehending, probably hostile and at best irrelevant to women's poetry is based on a perfectly accurate perception of most (male) criticism, it has the great benefit of enabling the feminist critic not to waste time and effort in countering prejudiced objections to the validity of women's claims to poetic distinction. Yet this dismissal of masculine thought and masculine tradition is sometimes made too easily – for these do, after all, constitute an enormously significant part of our intellectual context. And the tradition originated and dominated by men, with which women's poetry engages, is itself the site of intense intellectual and political struggle. To ignore this tradition means also ignoring women's struggle to transform its values. Admiration for the radical feminist practice and critique of poetry has to be qualified by the recognition that its vigour and consistency are too often achieved at the price of crucial oversimplifications.

To begin with a literary-critical point, the assumption that the significance of a poem is to be identified with the experience and consciousness of the poet is always debatable, because it is the poems which are available to us, not the poet's mind. Even though the poet's personality may seem to validate and explain her work, it remains a hypothesis which we construct out of the poems themselves plus any information we may have about the poet. (For a classic exposition of the arguments for the uncertainty of authorial intention, see the essay 'The Intentional Fallacy' by Wimsatt and Beardsley.)[10] It is impossible to read, say, Adrienne Rich's poem 'Frame' or Judy Grahn's 'A Woman is Talking to Death'[11] and not feel the strong pressure of feminist intention, but the poems of Emily Brontë or of H.D. are a very different proposition.

To read the women poets of the past and present for their covert or declared awareness of themselves as women is to lay a kind of grid of feminism over the map of poetry. Of course, this is in many respects a critical gain; for since women have throughout history endured oppression through their femaleness, and since women poets have written of this suffering with varying degrees of obliquity, bitterness or generosity, this grid at best enables the critic to read the map of poetry with a clear sense of direction and an enlarged richness of detail. But because if we stick exclusively to this grid we can read the map in no other way, the method makes for a finally limited critical practice. Graves's 'There is one story and one story only'[12] is a wonderful line but a warning to critics. And criticism based on the assumption that what makes a poem valuable and interesting is its author's awareness, enacted within it, of her own dilemma as a woman (which in practice generally means her sexual/ domestic life) risks reducing everything to the personal.

To read Sylvia Plath's poems for the way they show the poet to have been the emotional victim of patriarchy is not so different from reading them as evidence for the poet's father-fixation; in both cases, biography prevails over the poems. The question which such an assumption of the primacy of female experience in women's poems avoids asking is: What makes a poem different from autobiography, fictionalized or otherwise?

A poem is always a pattern of words, creating its particular meaning from the relation between the material reality of language – sounds, breathing, letters on a page – and the images and ideas which they signify. As Pasternak wrote, 'The music of the word ... does not consist of the euphony of vowels and consonants taken by themselves, but of the relationship between the meaning and the sound of words.'[13] This relationship, of course, exists wherever language is used. But it is the power of poetry, uniquely among forms of speech and writing, to manifest this relation, whether as pleasure or as paradox. So reading and listening to poetry always means keeping alert to the shape and feel of words, from the enjoyable reassurance of the refrains in nursery-rhymes to H.D.'s discontinuous, allusive meditations on words as simultaneously symbolic and material:

> and Venus as desire
> is venereous, lascivious,
>
> and the very root of the word shrieks
> like a mandrake when foul witches pull
>
> its stem at midnight,
> and rare mandragora itself
>
> is full, they say, of poison,
> food for the witches' den.[14]

No other kind of writing holds its own words up to the light as poetry does. To assume that poems are primarily ways into the poets' own experience means ignoring or at least underplaying the crucial significance of material formalities in creating poetic meaning, stressing instead a unity of consciousness with verbal expression.

Not that proponents of poetry as experience are necessarily indifferent to the intensities of poetic language. The way in which radical feminists understand these qualities can be seen when Lilian Mohin and Adrienne Rich both preface collections of women's poems with the claim that poetry is a potentially revolutionary medium for women because of its linguistic intensity, combined with its privileged relation to our consciousness. This is apparent when Lilian Mohin writes of the political possibilities of poetry, which 'with its tradition of concentrated insights, its brevity of form, is the ideal vehicle for the kind of politics we propose . . . Our work constitutes a challenge to the philosophical/religious constructs which underlie all human activity. Because women have not participated in deciding what is "right" or what is "real" or what is "natural", these controlling concepts have lacked an important reality and have oppressed us. Now we intend to expand, perhaps to burst all these ideas, and each small poem, each act of consciousness raising, is part of the great collective work.'[15] Similarly, Adrienne Rich insists on the links between poetic language, power and consciousness, when she writes in a preface to Judy Grahn's poems that 'Poetry is above all a concentration of the *power* of language, which is the power of our ultimate relation to everything in the universe . . . Think of the deprivation of women living for centuries without a poetry that spoke of women together, of women alone, of women as anything but the fantasies of men.'[16]

The excitement apparent in these conceptions of the political and linguistic possibilities of poetry is immensely attractive. But these possibilities are assumed, not explored; the writers seem to think of poetic intensity as a kind of electric charge, generated between the poles of the poet's mind and that of her reader or listener. The arguments of both women are validated not by an articulated theory but by the writing and editing of admirable feminist poems. (Rich is famous; Lilian Mohin, little known outside feminist circles, is also a fine poet.)[17] To say that Adrienne Rich and Lilian Mohin are more interested in writing politically committed poems of experience than in putting together a coherent feminist theory of poetic language is itself not, of course, a criticism; but it does point to a crucial absence in their thinking, which feminist critics who argue for a woman-centred language, based on their work,[18] have not dealt with. In Chapter 5, 'Female language and Imaginary identity', I discuss at length the question of a female poetic language, and the relation between women's poetry and female identity; meanwhile, this intuitive understanding of the language of poetry as emotionally and politically important, accompanied by no corresponding understanding of *how* that importance functions, represents for me both the strength and the shortcomings of radical feminist criticism. I am not suggesting that the method which sees this direct relation between 'poet as woman' and the poetry she produces is useless; on the contrary, it can be a valuable approach when used with justification and sparingly. But on its own, this method cannot carry the weight of feminist poetics.

2 Unrecognized Romanticism

It is not possible to discuss radical feminist poetics satisfactorily by keeping strictly within its political assumptions. For its central notion, that poetry articulates personal experience, is, though in many forms, common to most contemporary poets and critics, and, as Randall

Jarrell argued,[19] originates, like many of the defining characteristics of modern poetry, with the Romantics. The tenets of the Romantic discourse of poetry got their classic expression in Wordsworth's preface to the *Lyrical Ballads* (1800). This makes the following key points. First, that the poet is the transcendent representative of all humanity, his consciousness and sympathies being as comprehensive as possible: 'He is the rock of defence of human nature, an upholder and preserver, carrying everywhere with him relationship and love ... the poet binds together by passion and knowledge the vast empire of human society, as it is spread over the whole earth, and all over time.'[20] On the other hand, Wordsworth emphasizes the poet's kinship with humanity, saying that in his qualities of imagination and intelligence he differs not 'in kind from other men, but only in degree'.[21] Second, says Wordsworth, poetry deals with feeling and memory, 'it takes its origin from emotion recollected in tranquillity',[22] and takes all significant human experience for its province, including that of children or farm labourers, not previously considered legitimate subjects for serious poetry. Third, poetry should employ the simplest possible speech, 'the language really spoken by men',[23] this being the most fully human and therefore the most poetic form of utterance. This last is a radical approach which was attacked by Wordsworth's hostile critic Francis Jeffrey on the grounds that the words of 'ploughmen amd market-wenches', without education and therefore incapable of 'just taste and refined sentiments',[24] could have nothing to do with great poetry. A similar account of the poet as a 'man speaking to men',[25] but less intellectual and more visionary and rhetorical, was made by Walt Whitman in the preface to *Leaves of Grass* (1851), insisting on the democratic and poetic potential of the whole American nation.

The relation between the work that comes out of these beliefs about poetry and the poems and manifestos of radical feminism is, obviously, not one of straightforward similarity. The Romantic discourse of poetry, as briefly summarized here, is less likely to strike feminist readers as determining the ways in which women poets write (and in any case, the radical feminist poets whose work I am discussing plainly learnt their techniques from modernists, not Romantics), than as constituting major problems for women poets generally. These problems can be neatly exemplified by the definition of the poet as 'a man speaking to men', which silently excludes women from poetic speech, not because Wordsworth intends such exclusion but because he is unaware of it. Nor have women poets claimed the transcendent status of 'universal' subject which Romantic discourse accorded to the poet. The way in which, on the contrary, the myth of Romantic transcendence constituted a major difficulty for the ambitions of nineteenth-century women poets – a difficulty which only Emily Dickinson negotiated successfully – is the subject of Margaret Homans's admirable study of female Romantic poets, *Women Writers and Poetic Identity* (1980; see below, pp. 60–2). Feminist poets are much aware of the potential arrogance of claims to represent humanity:

> their generosity is presumptuous
> no one speaks to me on behalf of the world
> I am the world   as they are
> indigenous wildlife   see   like trees
> and dolphins   and children
> as innocent   as natural   and perhaps
> though I'm sure they can hardly stomach the thought
> more human   because   necessarily
> more consious
> think about that for awhile
> (Sheila Shulman, 'Hard Words, or why lesbians have to be philosophers')[26]

Although the poet's target here is actually heterosexual

liberals, her insistence on her own right to poetic self-definition can also be read as a refutation of Romantic claims to include and represent the world – as if one of the 'labourers going forth to till the fields'[27] on the margin of Wordsworth's vision spoke for herself: 'I am the world as they are.'

Nevertheless, radical feminist poetry and criticism are no less shaped by the inheritance of Romanticism than other kinds of modern poetry; shaped partly through the poets' and critics' struggles to escape or transform its assumptions, and partly because Romanticism underlies two aspects of the radical feminist aesthetic: its belief that poetry gives us privileged access to the (woman) poet's own experience, and that poetry is a form of transcendence – 'a concentration of the *power* of language, which is the power of our ultimate relation to everything in the universe'.[28] The Romantic myth of the great poet with his universal sympathies is replaced by a vision of multiple-authored poetry as a highly charged collective repository of female experience. Or to put it more concisely, the poet as 'man speaking to men' is transformed into a poetry of 'women speaking to each other'. This is apparent in, for instance, Lilian Mohin's introduction to the anthology of feminist poems *One Foot on the Mountain* (1979), quoted above, with its assertion of close links between poetry and consciousness-raising: 'We intend to tell each other everything we can because we know that this intimate, difficult exchange makes a difference, is the process of change';[29] or more figuratively in Adrienne Rich's collection *The Dream of a Common Language* (1978), which celebrates and elegizes a multitude of women, both famous and anonymous.

This unrecognized Romantic inheritance carries its problems for the poet, and still more for the critic, who bases her work on the assumptions of radical feminism as I have outlined them. It is not only that, as I argue above,

attention to the material, verbal aspects of poetry is liable
to disappear in the vicinity of the ideal – or fantasy – of
poetry as experience encountered at white heat. This is
apparent in the critic who writes of Rich's poetry: 'I have
to react [to it] viscerally, with my body. I feel the power of
her images, the impact of her use of temperatures, images of
tearing, cutting, shattering, of blood and semen, of sexual
ecstasy and sexual violence.'[30] More seriously, there are
also certain political evasions which, if not actually inherent
in the process of idealizing poetry as universal consciousness, are made very easy by it. The idea of his comprehensive
identity enabled the bourgeois male Romantic poet to be far
more humanly inclusive than his Augustan predecessors (as
the reactionary Jeffrey saw and deplored); but also, since
'he' represented all humanity, to avoid engaging with the
recalcitrant facts of class and gender. And similarly, the
tendency to privilege the notion of female experience, and
to think of women's poetry as a magically powerful
collective consciousness, can make for a too easy and
uncritical assumption of identity between all women: the
kind of assumption that has in political practice recently
been challenged by the articulate anger of Black women
who have found white feminists unable or unwilling to
acknowledge their experience of racist oppression as
relevant to their experience as women. I had wanted to
bring home this point with a quotation from the poem
'White Woman, Hey' by Carmen Williams,[31] denouncing a
white feminist for her failure to recognize Black women's
experience of racist oppression, and for her generally
patronizing attitudes. However, permission to print was
refused as the author did not want her poem printed in a
context of white literary criticism, however feminist: an
impasse which certainly illustrates the crucially differing
experiences and viewpoints of women of opposed cultures,
races and educations with particular clarity. Where
women's experiences do not match there can still, of course,
be communication – both sides can listen and speak – but

this is not likely to be easy; nor does it help to gloss the problem over by assertions of the unity of female experience.

This kind of insensitivity is not a political weakness that affects the radical feminist poets themselves; they have on the whole been generous champions of the oppressed, and much aware of their 'larger context of racial, economic and social inequality and struggle',[32] while the Romantic tendency to evade material contradictions by idealizing the possibilities of poetry affects critics[33] rather than creators. Poets have been much aware of the ambiguities of their work: a case in point is Irena Klepfisz's sequence of dramatic poems called 'Work Sonnets',[34] which explore the relationship of mutual curiosity, respect and incomprehension between the head of a typing pool and a much younger, presumably feminist woman who has taken employment as a typist in order (with some naivety) to find out about the lives of office workers. The narrative finishes with the older woman's angry refusal to co-operate in what she sees as the project of being defined by patronising intellectuals who have escaped her servitude. The effect of this outburst (which breaks off the sequence) is to subtly question the very project of representing, in a poem, the mind of a woman who half-realizes, bitterly, that she has lost her own creativity through becoming the skilful servant of other people's words (including perhaps the words of the poet). This self-irony is a matter of implication, of emphasis and of organization, and is not immediately apparent; it is possible because – as all students of literature learn – a poem's structure defines its meaning. Criticism has been less self-reflexive, and less sensitive.

But the point of my emphasizing that the origins of radical feminist poetry and criticism lie partly in Romanticism is not to blame poets and critics for being influenced by Romantic myths of universality without knowing it – though I do suggest that this misrecognition is made easier by radical feminists' tendency to disregard those aspects of poetry which are not specifically determined by women's consciousness and experience. For the Romantic tradition – among others – is still an inevitable part of the intellectual context of poetry today: no one can write poems without engaging with the complex of themes, images, myths, stereotypes, reference-points and conventions which are roughly denominated by the word 'tradition'. Even if a poet knows only the work of contemporaries, she will still be influenced by contemporary conventions of writing, including their residual Romanticism – and the more so, the less she is aware of the process.

3 Tradition and female identity

Literary traditions are, of course, often actively unhelpful to women poets working at once in and counter to them. It is a feminist commonplace now to say that the images and conventions of traditional English poetry are frequently demeaning to women[35] (though it is said less often that women poets enjoy a positive advantage in not being able to use stereotypes straightforwardly). And yet such demeaning or ambiguous representatives did and do overlap with the ways in which women understand themselves, and consequently affect women's poetry. This contradiction emerges with particular clarity from the study of women's love-poems, which I discuss at length in Chapter 4, and, with a different emphasis, in Chapter 5. It is an assumption of our culture that sexuality is the area where the self is most profoundly known and defined; it is also conventional, in a much cruder way, for women to be defined through their sexuality according to the stereotyped opposition of virtuous virgin to sexy whore. This convention distorts the reality of female desire, but because it is so widespread, it is virtually impossible for women to define their own sexuality without reference to it, however oblique. But, of course, the enormous majority of women's love-poems were not written as consciously feminist articulations of female sexuality; and – to assume for the moment that poetry and self-expression are interchangeable – when women do write poems out of and about their own desire, there is no need or pressure for them to reproduce the conventions of the masculine poem which represents Woman as the object of male sexual fantasy. On the other hand, the simple opposition 'men's poems = masculine stereotype: false' versus 'women's poems = female experience: true' does not correspond to the actuality of women's poems. For example, the sonnets of Edna St Vincent Millay and Christina Rossetti (discussed at length in Chapter 4), and of Elizabeth Barrett Browning, are visibly the work of women poets inserting themselves into a traditionally masculine form: namely, the sonnet sequence dramatizing and meditating on a love relationship. The subversion of traditional form and meaning which is implied in the poet's being of the gender conventionally ascribed to muse not to maker, produces in these poems a criticism, whether overt or only implied, of traditional stereotypes. But to criticize tradition is not to be disconnected from it, so that we would not truly understand these poems by looking in them for evidence of a purely female discourse of sexuality. Christina Rossetti's sonnets, for example, are certainly affected in complex ways by their assent to the Victorian axiom that virtuous love must be a hundred per cent chaste. In other words, the question 'How do these poems articulate a female sexual identity?' cannot be answered satisfactorily without raising the differently angled questions: 'How do these women poets engage with the conventions within which they practise? Do they transform them, or evade them, or do neither?'

The depth and complexity of women poets' engagement with masculine tradition can be seen by looking at some examples of the way a traditional motif is handled by different women poets. The motif I have chosen is flower-imagery (that hardy perennial of the English lyric). It is a classic instance of imagery whose feminine connotations are very common, at once attractive and demeaning. Flowers, particularly roses, have a time-honoured association with female sexuality; they traditionally symbolize women's beauty and vulnerability to decay ('Beauty is but a flower / Which wrinkles will devour').[36] While such symbolism is not obviously sexist, it is, in Cora Kaplan's phrase, 'subliminally degrading',[37] in that it makes woman represent all that is most transient and pleasurable (for man). In 'Hybrid Perpetual', Lucy Boston makes this symbolism the centre of a poem whose description of a flower unfolding is also a sexual metaphor:

> . . . And though some say that love outlasts the heart
> As if the perfume were not of the flower,

> It is enough that the rose comes out of darkness
> Rich with the dew that slakes it,
> Acquiescent and ardent,
> Opening its golden coronal
> As the sun unmakes it.[38]

It is clear that this 'acquiescent and ardent' rose is female; indeed, the poem points up its own sexual symbolism ('When the dark rose is open / And dew rolls in each cleft / Moist in the diamond morning')[39] with a boldness which is in strong tension with its fastidious but fairly conventional poetic diction and very literary form, both of which invite the reader to bear in mind its classical predecessors Ronsard, Spenser, Waller and Blake.[40] Lucy Boston thus uses traditional symbolism to represent an intense sexuality ignored or played down by her literary great-uncles, for whom the flower conventionally represented their pleasure, not its own ecstasy. Furthermore, she makes this symbol the medium of a 'universal' truth: brevity is the condition of *all* delight. But one cannot take this as a feminist poem, since its flower-symbolism is profoundly affected by the traditional associations of passivity and fragility with femininity. The sexuality celebrated here is far from autonomous; it exists as a response to the sun's penetrating light and heat.

The sexual symbolism of flowers is even more overt in Sylvia Plath's dramatic monologue 'Poppies in July':

Little poppies, little hell flames,
Do you do no harm?

You flicker. I cannot touch you.
I put my hands among your flames. Nothing burns.

And it exhausts me to watch you
Flickering like that, wrinkly and clear red, like the
    skin of a mouth.

A mouth just bloodied.
Little bloody skirts![41]

In this poem, the speaker's agonized tone and rapid changes of imagery make the (really very conventional) associations of poppies – red cupped flowers – with female sexuality appear to be a projection of her own fantasy. Thus, her vision of the blooms as bloodied mouths and 'little bloody skirts' suggests that she is imagining a whorish lipsticked, perhaps bruised mouth, and bleeding genitals: menstruation, defloration or violent rape are evoked. Her wondering whether the poppies might burn her recalls, though surely not intentionally, Charlotte Mew's 'The Quiet House', whose speaker is likewise close to derangement:

And a rose can stab you across the street
    Deeper than any knife
And the crimson haunts you everywhere[42]

The speaker of 'Poppies in July', obsessed by jealousy,

associates the poppies with the idea of her rival in the act of sexual possession. The poem ends with a fantasy of extracting from the poppies their traditional essence of oblivion, without their troubling redness: 'Or your liquors seep to me . . . dulling and stilling. / But colourless. Colourless.'[43] Plath's poem could be read as an oblique gloss on Iago's gloat: 'Not poppy nor mandragora / Nor all the soothing syrups of the world / Shall ever medicine thee to that sweet sleep.'[44] Yet the poem has no easy commerce with poetic tradition: because its speaker is so obsessive, and the logic of her mind (which bounds the poem) is associative, not rational, it is easy to see that its symbolism is arbitrary, and hard to see that its arbitrariness is in truth traditionally determined. Conventional meanings are pushed to a savage, almost unrecognizable extreme, and yet are apparent in the disturbing representation of female sexuality as a whorish bloody mouth.

Alison Fell's poem 'Girl's gifts', in contrast, reads as written outside the traditional poetic context invoked by these poems of sexuality:

> I glance across the grass
> a shadow in the window is my mother
> cooking, watching.
> I am making a tiny secret basket for my grandmother.
> My mouth waters.
> I would lick the green leaf, taste the bronze
> and yellow silk of the snapdragon.
> I mould petals, weave stems, with love,
> my little finger inches in the folds:
> it is done, red and gold.
>
> I will carry it cupped like a jewel or a robin's egg
> It will lie, perfect, in her wrinkled palm
> I will cross the grass and give it.[45]

This poem is, however unobtrusively, feminist. The flower-basket is a gift from a child, watched by her mother, to her grandmother: the poem's social world is one of women, giving, nurturing and protecting. The gift of the flower-basket recalls Katherine Mansfield's story 'Prelude' in which the little girl Kezia makes arrangements of flowers in empty matchboxes, called 'surprises', for her grandmother.[46] The flowers themselves are neither sexualized nor fragile: they survive both the little girl's sensuality, expressed in touching and tasting, and her weaving and modelling operations. A child's flower-basket is itself the antithesis of an artistic monument 'more enduring than bronze';[47] as Adrienne Rich writes in a very similar context, 'Such a composition has nothing to do with externity.'[48] Flower arranging is usually practised by women: it is a short-term, decorative art, not highly regarded. The poem thus represents itself as part of women's culture of making, sharing and enjoying, in which the process of creation is valued more than the artefact. Yet even the kind of feminist culture suggested here does not exist entirely without reference to the formal magnificence which is, implicitly, rejected. The poem contests, however obliquely, the slight value traditionally set on women's occupations, finding a central importance in what had been relegated to the marginal: what it does not do is speak 'outside' tradition. Alison Fell's use of the monologue is a characteristically 'modern' form, while a Romantic inheritance is apparent in the way the child's perceptions, as much as or more than her actions, focus the poem. The difference lies in the unobtrusive but firm emphasis on specifically female creativity.

What emerges from these analyses, then, is that even in the most overtly casual, feminist poem, the flowers are not innocently 'there', devoid of the traditional symbolism which determines the limit of their possible meanings. In other words, tradition appears as determining in the way it defines the symbolic and referential context of the poems, and not necessarily as a product of the poet's own intention. It would be good to read these poems as part of a specific tradition of women's poetry. The parallels I've drawn between Plath and Mew, Fell and Mansfield, are intended as contributions to this possibility. But this cannot be imagined as a simple tradition of female intelligence at work on otherwise undefined material. I do not mean that (re)constructing such a women's tradition would mean nothing more than noting and analysing the ways in which women have used and modified masculine themes and symbols – this would be a dispiritingly modest proposal, especially after emphasizing the determining power of such themes. Still less do I mean that women poets ought to avoid 'traditional' imagery so as not to get tangled up in masculine definitions. My point is rather that poetic tradition needs to be seen not only as a defining context, but as an area of perpetual struggle, both political and intellectual.

4 Women's exclusion: a cautionary tale

Although traditions originated by men are, as we have seen, deeply influential on women's writing, the radical feminist perception that these are alien to women holds an indispensable truth. As readers and writers we may inherit the past and share the general preoccupations of the present, but as women we do not officially belong to the traditions that may engage us. The irony and difficulty of our relation to the common literary inheritance can be illuminated by taking a careful look at a particular instance of the way women are excluded from the construction of a tradition. My example is the still-continuing history of the critical reception of English poets and novelists of the 1930s; and although the exclusions from the canon of significant texts which I detail here are mostly of prose writers, rather than poets, this story of the critical reception – or rather nonreception – of women's writing is relevant to the problems of poetry.

The history of Britain in the 1930s, which begins with financial catastrophe and ends in world war, has meant that the events of that decade have been much worked over by historians and critics: there are ten book-length studies of its literature alone.[49] Literary analyses of the young writers of the thirties, notably Auden and Spender, who publicly identified themselves with the Left, and sometimes with the Communist Party, have taken two main directions. In the 1950s and 1960s, the usual version was that the intellectual life of Britain and Europe had been dominated by left-wing liberals – 'starry-eyed do-gooders with pink illusions'[50] – more or less ignorantly under the control of the Communist Third International. An important source for this view is the collection of recanting essays by ex-Communist intellectuals, *The God That Failed*.[51] A different, more nuanced understanding of Auden, Spender and co. in terms of their subjectivity became possible with the publication of Robin Skelton's Penguin anthology *Poetry of the 1930s* (1964), which made a mass of previously arcane material easily available. Skelton's choice and arrangement of the poems, as well as his introductory essay, defined the 'poetry of the 1930s' as manifesting the preoccupations of a particular generation of middle-class intellectuals. His emphasis on the personal and emotional side of this politically committed poetry was extended to prose fiction and essays by Samuel Hynes's influential *The Auden Generation* (1976), which inaugurated a decade of readings of the young writers of the thirties in terms of their characteristic imagery and mythologies. The theme of Hynes's book is the way the 'Auden generation' constructed autobiographical parables and semi-private mythologies to negotiate their relationship to public, political crises, including the historic trauma of the Great War, as well as the rise of fascism.

All very interesting, but what (readers may ask) has any of it to do with women? The answer according to the standard histories is: Virtually nothing. Skelton's anthology *Poetry of the Thirties* includes one woman poet, Anne Ridler, and the introductory essay mentions Edith Sitwell as the butt of the progressive literary reviews.[52] Sitwell and Sylvia Townsend Warner each rate a sneer, the latter anonymously, from Julian Symons's *The Thirties: A Dream Revolved* (1975).[53] Samuel Hynes mentions no women poets, but five novelists: Elizabeth Bowen, Rosamond Lehmann, Storm Jameson, Naomi Mitchison and Virginia Woolf – all named only as reviewers or correspondents of the young male writers.[54] Bernard Bergonzi's *Reading the Thirties* (1978) mentions three middlebrow women novelists – Agatha Christie, Vicki Baum and Barbara Lucas – and in the chapter 'Icon or Commodity?' discusses several women film stars including Garbo and Hepburn.[55] The record of the Left is not much better: *The 1930s: A Challenge to Orthodoxy* (ed. John Lucas, 1978) failed to challenge sexual orthodoxy, none of its essays being addressed to the work of women poets or novelists,[56] while *Practices of Literature and Politics* (ed. Francis Barker, 1979) is equally a blank on women, though its accompanying volume, *The Politics of Modernism*, does include papers on Virginia Woolf and Dorothy Richardson. The only attention accorded to the work of any woman poet that I have found in all this critical literature is the brief discussion and assessment of Kathleen Raine in A.J. Tolley's *Poetry of the Thirties* (1975).[57]

This absence of women from critical history is not because of a corresponding absence of relevant material. Women writers – and not only those mentioned above – produced important work in this period, which dealt with the same themes which have been expounded by the literary histories of Symons, Hynes and Bergonzi. Obvious candidates for any critical work dealing with the literary-social history of the 1930s are Vera Brittain, Winifred Holtby, Jean Rhys, Sylvia Townsend Warner and Antonia White. All of these responded creatively to the social and political issues of the time in ways which are closely, though not always directly, related to the characteristic preoccupations of the male 'Auden Generation', including both their left-wing politics and their tendency to autobiography. The fact that their work is nearly all fiction does not explain its exclusion: all the books I have mentioned include discussions of prose writing. (Richard Johnstone's study of 1930s fiction, *The Will to Believe* (1982) discusses no woman novelist.) The evident similarities between the preoccupations of these middle-class women and the young male writers is not surprising, for these women shared the same social position as members of a fairly homogeneous upper-middle class, and therefore knew the same literary culture as well as living through the same history.* Thus, Stevie Smith's *Novel on Yellow Paper* (1936) includes a disgusted account of a visit to Nazi Germany that should be read alongside Isherwood's *Goodbye to Berlin* (1939); and when she sent her heroine into a world of spying and melodrama in *Over the Frontier* (1938) she deployed that myth of

---

*Schools are a quick guide to British social class. The best-known writers of the 1930s – Auden, Isherwood, Greene, Spender, MacNeice, Orwell, Day Lewis, Waugh – all went to public schools, and all but Orwell to Oxford or Cambridge afterwards.[58] Of the women in my list, Vera Brittain and Winifred Holtby were educated at Somerville College, Oxford; Stevie Smith attended the North London Collegiate School, and Jean Rhys the Perse School for Girls, Cambridge – both schools belonging to the Girls' Public Day schools Trust. Antonia White went to the school of the Convent of the Sacred Heart. All of these are solid academic institutions: anyone who attended them got a share, though a comparatively inexpensive one, of educational privilege. Sylvia Townsend Warner, who had no institutional education but a highly cultivated home, also shared the same educational background and privileges.

frontiers and borderlines which Professor Hynes and Bergonzi see as classic 'Audenesque parable'. In a more overtly political context, Vera Brittain's pacifist memoir of the Great War *Testament of Youth* (1933), and Virginia Woolf's analysis of the relation between militarism and masculinity in *Three Guineas* (1938) both contributed to pacifist thinking – politically widespread in the thirties – and, more obliquely, to anti-war mythology. Jean Rhys's novels *After Leaving Mr Mackenzie* (1936) and *Good Morning, Midnight* (1938) have a bitter urban poetry that is both like and unlike the Greeneland of *England Made Me* (1938), *Brighton Rock* (1936) and *A Gun For Sale* (1935). Winifred Holtby's *South Riding* (1935), which delineates the effects of the economic slump on the lives of individuals in a small community, is comparable in its much more optimistic, middle-class way with Greenwood's *Love on the Dole* (1932). The most striking of these exclusions is the near-total silence in literary histories about the poet and novelist Sylvia Townsend Warner, whose novels *Summer Will Show* (1936) and *After the Death of Don Juan* (1939) are still out of print. Though the years 1930–1940 must be one of the most written-up decades of modern poetry, literary analyses have never covered her poems, and her appearance in the standard histories is virtually limited to Spender's unnamed caricature of 'a Communist lady writer and her friend, a lady poet'[59] at the writers' congress in Madrid in 1937 in his memoir *World Within World* (1953), quoted with approval by Julian Symons.[60] The irony of this is that Sylvia Townsend Warner's life corresponds in many respects to the standard biography of a progressive intellectual in the thirties (father a Harrow schoolmaster; homosexual; joins the Communist Party in 1935; publishes Marxist poems; goes to Republican Spain during the Civil War; works on the editorial committee of *Left Review*) – but, as a woman, these sexual and political commitments leave her invisible or, if noticed, ludicrous. Spender's sexual double standard is obvious here: his own relationship with 'Jimmy Younger' is presented in *World Within World* as, however unsatisfactory, a serious matter, whereas a lesbian couple is regarded as good for a laugh. The work of Auden, Spender and Isherwood is itself noticeably misogynist, haunted as their plays, poems and novels are by devouring or vengeful mother-figures, with an occasional sexy temptress to give light relief.[61] One can detect an uncanny reappearance of these figures as mild and attenuated shades in the critics' rerun of the drama of the Auden Generation, in which women are assigned a few walk-on parts as intellectual nannies (Bowen, Woolf and Mitchison nurturing the Young Hopefuls in the literary reviews), unreverend mothers (Sitwell) or beautiful faces (Garbo), but female experience and writing are ignored.

I do not, of course, accuse Professors Hynes, Bergonzi and the rest of deliberate omission. As is all too plain, it simply never occurred to them that anything by women could be relevant (except perhaps as commentary) to the politico-literary myths they describe, whose assumptions they unconsciously reproduce. This is not because any of the relevant material by women is obscure: all the titles I mention, except for the Warner novels, are currently in print, thanks partly to feminist publishing houses; and many of them have already received critical attention. But this attention has never included any considering of women, in their own right, as contributors to 'thirties writing'. A woman's place is still *not* thought to be that intersection of public and private life where major literature is supposed to be constructed. This critical neglect of women's writing confirms my contention that literary tradition needs to be understood not only as a defining context but – especially for women – as an area of political and intellectual struggle. It is that struggle which is the subject of the following chapters.

CHAPTER 2

WOMEN AND TRADITION

1 The paradoxes of exclusion

'Wooman, lovely Wooman', said Mr Turveydrop, with very disagreeable gallantry. 'What a sex you are!'[1]

Women have a paradoxical relationship to tradition. As readers and writers, we belong to it, but as women we are excluded. The body of work which constitutes the canon of English literature as taught in schools and universities, is nearly all written by and for men, displays masculine preoccupations, and usually either ignores women or presents us as stereotypes which usually invoke variants of the familiar angel/whore dichotomy.

Our exclusion, then, takes the forms of misinterpretation and of simple omission. I have already discussed the latter in section 4 ('Women's exclusion') of Chapter 1; this chapter is concerned with the trickier question of misrepresentation and the difficulties this creates for the woman poet. I do not, however, mean here to detail and analyse the ways in which traditional, stereotypical representations of women repress or distort our actual reality. The project of deconstructing masculine representations of women has been a vitally important task undertaken by feminist criticism, from Kate Millett's pioneering *Sexual Politics* (1968) to Luce Irigaray's deconstructive *Speculum* (1974) or Rosalind Coward's deciphering of the politics of commercial representations of women in *Female Desire* (1985). The richness and analytic strength of this work means that feminists can today take the misrepresentation of woman in traditional stereotypes as given. What I explore here is women poet's difficult relationship to this authoritative but frustrating tradition; how they negotiate their paradoxical exclusion; and how they write at once within and in spite of the context of a defining poetic tradition in which their gender makes them seem 'naturally' the bearers of others' meanings.

One way of approaching the problem of tradition is to see it as a personal dilemma faced by all women writers. This emphasis on the poet's personal struggle appears in two influential texts, the first by Adrienne Rich and the second by Sandra Gilbert and Susan Gubar. In 'When We Dead Awaken: Writing as Re-vision', Adrienne Rich writes of the young woman poet:

> [The] girl or woman . . . tries to write because she is peculiarly susceptible to language. She goes to poetry or fiction looking for *her* way of being in the world, since she too has been putting words and images together; she is looking eagerly for guides, maps, possibilities; and over and over again in the words' 'masculine persuasive force' of literature she comes up against something that negates everything she is about: she meets the image of Woman in books written by men. She finds a terror and a dream, she finds a beautiful pale face, she finds La Belle Dame Sans Merci, she finds Juliet or Tess or Salome, but precisely what she does not find is that absorbed, drudging, puzzled, sometimes inspired creature, herself, who sits at a desk trying to put words together.[2]

The male poets' image of Woman 'negates everything [the woman writer] is about', not only because it does not fit her experience, but because of its usual connotations of uncreative passivity. Rich has written of this, brilliantly, in an early poem:

> When to her lute Corinna sings
> neither words nor music are her own,
> only the long hair dipping
> over her cheek, only the song
> of silk against her knees
> and these
> adjusted in reflections of an eye.[3]

This poetic gloss on Thomas Campion's lyric[4] points out that 'Corinna' doesn't compose; her 'song' is her lovely appearance. And for Rich to designate the woman idealized in song as 'Corinna' is a highly appropriate irony, for it is the name of an ancient Greek woman poet whose works have disappeared even more completely than Sappho's. 'Corinna' thus stands for the double exclusion of women from poetry: by omission and by (mis)representation. Emphasizing the alienation experienced by a woman poet encountering a tradition full of Corinnas, Rich makes that experience representative; her eloquent description is a kind of exemplary fable, which personifies the problem of tradition in the woman poet's struggles to escape the image of herself generated by patriarchal texts.

A similar exemplary fable of the pains of female creativity at once governs and energizes Sandra Gilbert and Susan Gubar's monumental study of women writers, *The Madwoman in the Attic* (1979). The right of women to verbal creation is the stake in the conflict with patriarchal authority which this book both chronicles and enacts; and the problem of tradition is represented, at the outset of the book, by a retelling of the story of Snow White in which the Wicked Queen becomes a doomed feminist heroine, rebelling against the constraints of the (mostly invisible) patriarchal king. This fable of the woman writer, the story of whose life is typically determined by an internal conflict between the perfect daughter of patriarchy and her stepmother and alter ego, the wicked queen, is used to interpret a multiplicity of poets and novelists. The story of the woman writer is the story of how the Queen, 'a plotter, an artist, an impersonator, a woman of almost infinite creative energy, witty, wily and self-absorbed as artists traditionally are',[5] attempts to kill her passive, beautiful enemy by 'the traditionally female arts of tight lacing, cosmetology and cuisine, but her three "plots" succeed only in transforming her rival into the eternally beautiful, intimate object d'art preserved in the glass coffin of patriarchal aesthetics';[6] the artist herself ending up by doing the death-dance in red-hot shoes, condemned under patriarchy to monstrosity and self-destruction.

In deploying this allegory of the woman writer's struggle against the deathly role of image assigned to her by tradition, the authors insist on the artist's need for autonomous self-definition: 'Before women can even attempt that pen which is so rigorously kept from them, they must escape just those male texts which, defining them as "Cyphers", deny them the authority to formulate alternatives to an authority which has imprisoned them and kept them from attempting the pen.'[7] The desire of the writer is to 'dance out of the looking-glass of the male text into a tradition that enabled her to create her own authority';[8] the work of the book thus consists in decoding the suppressed evidence of 'hunger, rebellion and rage'[9] in classic female texts.

Sandra Gilbert and Susan Gubar deal mostly with fiction, arguing that poetry is appallingly problematic for women: 'verse genres have been even more thoroughly male than fictional ones'.[10] For example, 'the sonnet, beginning with Petrarch's celebrations of "his" Laura, took shape as a poem in praise of the poet's mistress, who . . . can never herself be a poet because she "is" poetry'.[11] Their implication that this form, like the equally male ode, [12] elegy or satire, constitutes an insuperable difficulty for the woman poet is, obviously, not literally true. While the sonnet has not been a favourite genre with women poets, those who did practise the form seriously have excelled as creators of sonnet sequences from the sixteenth to the twentieth century.[13] What the argument insists on is the psychological difficulty of such success: it implies that, for example, Christina Rossetti must have experienced anxiety at her own transgressive action when she gave a poetic voice to Petrarch's muse in the 'Monna Innominata' sonnets, and may perhaps have wondered whether she ought to have confined herself to modelling as a saint in her brother's paintings.[14] The appropriate reading of these sonnets would then be a deciphering of the anxiety which Christina Rossetti must have felt at her own daring, and her anger at being able to dare so little in a genre which was itself a kind of psychic prison. But although, as my discussion of these sonnets in Chapter 4 ('Two-Way Mirrors' pp. 125–34) finds, these poems offer plenty of evidence of constriction and concomitant resentment, these derive from the sonnets' narrative *donnée* of deprivation, reinforced by Victorian ideologies of 'virtuous' love, not from the form – though its restrictions certainly tighten the screw. If the sonnet-form really had been hopelessly recalcitrant, Rossetti's contemporary Elizabeth Barrett Browning should not have been able to produce the *Sonnets from the Portuguese*, a sequence which does, with whatever limitations, narrate a story of emotional release.

It should also be pointed out here how much a critic's own (re)construction of tradition plays a major part in the way she interprets and values texts. This can be seen plainly when feminist critics come independently to opposite conclusions about the same subject. This happens when Tillie Olsen, in *Silences* (1979), quotes with sympathy Gerard Manley Hopkins's anguished accounts of his writer's block in terms of castration, whereas in *The Madwoman in the Attic* Gilbert and Gubar attack Hopkins for using just these metaphors, which presuppose that creativity and fertility are the prerogative of the penis.[15] For the socialist Tillie Olsen, interested in the material conditions for (and impediments to) writing, the apparent failure of Hopkins, unpublished during his lifetime and producing comparatively few poems, makes him a fellow victim of blocked and discouraged women writers whom her book rescues, at least in part, from the silence that stifled them. For Gilbert and Gubar, Hopkins the man is less significant than his commanding posthumous presence, which is certainly very powerful among critics and teachers of poetry; consequently, he is for them one of the arch oppressors.

It will be clear from these arguments and objections that I find the approach to the problem of women's relation to poetic tradition which sees this primarily as a psychological problem, somewhat limited. This is partly because the Romantic conception of the writer alone with her words and thoughts, which this approach implies, does not take enough account of the material conditions which make it possible for women to write (or, in many cases, prevent them from doing so). To me, the obvious common-sense objections that having the time and space to write in, being able to talk or at least correspond with fellow-writers, and having access to the means of publication, however limited, are more influential than the deterrent effects of Milton, Wordsworth and Co., carry a lot of weight. They are, incidentally, confirmed by the success of feminist writing collectives, which demand the first condition and supply the others.[16] And the critical methods implied by these exemplary fables of the woman writer struggling with the wraiths generated by patriarchal tests, are potentially reductive, leading as they logically do to definitions of all women's writing in terms of this same wounding, heroic struggle. It seems to me that, by contrast, the problems of tradition exist not so much for the poet as for the poem. By this I mean that the difficulties of creating women's meanings in forms and symbols which presuppose them as the bearers not the makers of significance, do not lie primarily in the experience of composition – not that this is ever easy. What matters is the symbolic and intellectual context which the individual poem implies, and which itself influences the way poems are understood. This point emerged in a simple way from the three poems by Lucy Boston, Sylvia Plath and Alison Fell, discussed in Chapter 1 (pp. 16–20), all of which are successful as poems and all of which are marked, in different ways, by the stereotyping associated with their deployment of flower imagery.

Yet to insist on the power of patriarchal definitions, without conceding the possibility of transforming them, means thinking of the woman poet as in thrall to them, like the speaker of Sylvia Plath's poem 'The Colossus', whose criticism is muted to self-irony:

> Scaling little ladders with gluepots and pails of Lysol
> I crawl like an ant in mourning
> Over the weedy acres of your brow
> To mend the immense skull-plates and clear
> The bald white tumuli of your eyes.[17]

It is true that, even in this example, there is a significant difference between the helpful drudgery implied by the combined domestic and archaeological metaphors, and the act of writing a poem about one's obsessional, disrespectful relation to a dead but still impressive tradition – perhaps also getting irony from the oblique allusion to Shelley's 'Ozymandias', another poem about a shattered colossus which is an impotent relic of tyranny. Yet the position is an unappealing one, and is certainly no more to be taken as the archetype of the woman poet's dilemma than the critical fables of her lonely struggle for self-definition, which do at least allow for the possibility of hope and change. The complexities of association and suggestion which arise from reading women's poems, imply that the individual poet's ambitions are finally less important than the arduous prospect of women transforming the symbolic order; or at least that portion of it which constitutes our poetic context.

2 'Transcending gender': Anne Stevenson

Many critics would see the problems entailed in women's relation to poetic tradition as non-existent and insignificant. These women (and men too, it goes without saying) would agree with Elizabeth Hardwick that 'every artist is either a woman or a man, and the struggle is pretty much the same for both',[18] and would sympathize with Joyce Oates's distaste at being classified as a 'woman writer'.[19] These women, equally wary of being dismissed into intellectual limbo by the patronising inattention of Mr Turveydrop the Traditionalist, and of being appropriated to Female Gothic by Mrs Jellyby the Jailer, would contend that there is only one tradition worth acknowledging: namely, that of humane writing, whoever produces it. The writer whom I have chosen to represent the view that humane writing is or should be free of gender considerations is the poet Anne Stevenson, whose literary criticism takes this line; as, more obliquely, do her poems. In the essay 'Writing as a Woman', she refuses the title of 'feminist poet':

> For better or worse, women and men writers in the
> West, in the later twentieth century, share a common
> consciousness. Their language is a reflection, or even a
> definition, of that consciousness. If anything we want
> *more* understanding, more communication between the
> sexes . . . If there is to be a new creative consciousness
> – one that is not based on the phallic values of

conquest, power, ambition, greed, murder and so on –
then this consciousness must have room for both male
and female – a consciousness that the greatest literature
has, in fact, been defining for a long time now.[20]

With its echoes of marriage vows co-existing uneasily
with a feminist critique of 'phallic values', this seems to
me troubled writing. But the argument against specifically
female discourse – 'writing as a woman' – is clear
enough. A more recent essay by Anne Stevenson is on the
poetry of Carol Rumens – 'one of the few women poets
writing today whose seriousness is absolute but not
closed'.[21] Praising Carol Rumens for the impersonal
sympathy of 'Outside Oswiecim' (a poem about a death
camp), she writes that 'her commitment is not to
Feminism or Socialism or any going dogma. She takes
responsibility for individual humanity within the general
horror'.[22] This humanist equation of the aesthetically
great with the non-political strikes me as itself a dogma,
and an extremely questionable one (where, for example,
does it leave a poem like Brecht's 'To Those Born
Later'?). But the significance of Anne Stevenson's insistence
on an ideal tradition of poetry informed by a contemplative consciousness shared by both sexes, is clearly
connected with the preoccupations of her own poems, in
which (as with most poets) her most interesting and
nuanced thinking is to be found. Her own most ambitious
work, such as 'Black Mountain, Green Mountain',
consists of meditation on the theme of national tradition,
and the passive but important role taken by women in the
living out of such tradition in the histories of people's
lives. This is apparent in her best-known – and most
feminist – book *Correspondences* (1974), a fragmentary
history of a bourgeois New England family called the
Chandlers, told through imaginary letters, diaries and
poems between 1828 and 1968. The story focuses mainly
on women, particularly the constraints they endure and

the limited options they can choose. The Chandler men are the professionals and achievers; significantly, their writings are nearly all in prose. Meanwhile, their women, a series of poets *manquées* (at least until the 1960s), produce a terse poetry of intellectual energy at work on a bleakly unrewarding domesticity:

> Youth from Harvard
> in exchange here, sprawled by the one fire
> bawling for malmscy, concocting us morsels
> for tomorrow's theological banquet while we
> shiver on his polar side, hungry for the supper
> our wet coals smoke but won't cook![23]

This quotation from Abigail Chandler's letter to her sister is typical of *Correspondences*' feminine poetic discourse of concise secret dissent. The Chandler men, conversely, run to prosy pomposity. Thus Jacob Chandler, putting pressure on his daughter Maura to drop her claims to independence and to literary ambition, demands that she return to the bosom of her family:

> Maura! Maura! Those kisses were never gifts!
> Bestowed with the charity of Our Lord Himself, those
> kisses were loans! Loans upon interest, these many long
> years! Now it is time to repay them, graciously,
> selflessly, with little acts of kindness and
> understanding.[24]

This unctuous emotional blackmail of course pays off, and within four years Maura is dutifully embarking, 'with little hope, / with no glad energy' on marriage to the worthy Ethan Boyd. But this etiolated rectitude begins to collapse in the next generation: Maura's daughter Ruth Arbeiter (whose name, appropriately for an epigone of Puritanism, means 'worker') also settles, though with some adulterous compromise, for marriage and respectability. Her affair with a literary English gent (whose plummy complacency and pretentious writing do not seem to put her off), and the poems inspired by this liaison, both remain unpublished. Her daughter Katherine, by contrast, abandons a wretched marriage and her own child to move from America to London as the poet 'Kay Boyd'. The price of the Chandlers' virtuous Victorian prosperity was the narrow, hypocritical complacency of the Chandler men and the frustrations endured by their wives and daughters; by the end of the book, neither Kay nor her brother Nick, whose only appearance is as a drop-out from college heading West (where else?) in 1968, composing poems *en route*, will pay this price. The price of their poetic liberation is the final bankruptcy of the tradition of New England Puritanism, of which they should have been heirs.

The experiences and viewpoints of women are central to this story. This can partly be explained by the poet's decision to narrate a century and a half of American history as a fragmentary domestic chronicle, which would anyway tend to foreground the traditionally feminine preoccupation with the personal and private. The Civil War, for instance, is only mentioned in one letter, and even there the national crisis appears mainly as an occasion for intra-family conflict – 'From this day forward I hate every Yank as my Father.'[25] But though *Correspondences* does make an implicitly feminist critique of New England, and though women get given nearly all its best lines, Anne Stevenson is clearly interested at least as much in the masculine Puritan tradition as in the women whose self-sacrifices make its contradictions possible. And both sexes live out its compromises and final breakdown.

These preoccupations surface again in a later poem, 'Black Mountain, Green Mountain', which plays off a British landscape (the Black Mountains in Wales) with an American one (the Vermont countryside). Overtly though allusively autobiographical, the poem meditates on the relation between national destiny and family history; thus the poet's journey homewards across the Atlantic 'with two trays full of cellophane food / and a B film',[26] recalls by contrast the memory of the Pilgrim Fathers travelling in the same direction 'to be the letter of the place / the page of the Lord's approval'.[27] Once again, it is the theme of domesticity which roots the spare, abstract meditation of the poem in reality:

> If you, mother, had survived
> you would have written . . .

> As when we were children
>   and everything was going on
>   forever in New Haven

> you scratched in your journal
>   *It is a strange reaction but*
>   *suddenly the war has made it*
>   *imperative to spend time*
>   *reading and being with my children.*

> The pen drew its meanings
>   through vacancy
>   threading a history.[28]

The daughter's meditation transforms into poetry her mother's record of her only partly conscious instinct ('It is a strange reaction') to keep alive humane culture and family love during an evil time. But I do not think that this passage can be taken as a straightforward affirmation of female values. Its 'women's world' of domesticity and cultivation comes over as valuable, but limited compared with the wider world of public issues, symbolized by the legends of the Pilgrim Fathers (and of Arthur's knights) which constitute its context in the poem.

It is clear from Anne Stevenson's poems as well as her criticism that she thinks of women's writing, including her own, not as part of a female culture (which she evidently associates, perhaps too narrowly, with domesticity) but as one aspect of the great tradition which is inherited by all readers along with their language, nationality and education. (It is true that this means taking her meditations on the Puritan tradition in America to represent her understanding of literary and poetic tradition in general as common to both sexes, but in view of the way she has defined this tradition in her essays, I don't think this is misleading.) The intellectual strength of her insistence that the tradition she belongs to transcends gender, lies in her refusal to be, as she sees it, ghettoized. Her weakness – as with most proponents of this argument – is that she idealizes the tradition which she endorses, failing to take account of the exclusions and injustices which help to constitute it, especially the marginalization of women's poetry. As was apparent in the example of the literary historians of the 1930s and their neglect of women's writing, expounded in Chapter 1 (pp. 20–5), women do *not* normally get included either in the canon of important literature or in reconstructions of that complex of feeling, myth and experience which makes up ideological traditions of the kind that Anne Stevenson's own poems explore. Her argument for the transcending of gender takes too little account of reality, assuming that major battles which are still in progress have already been won. Certainly, there is an obvious irony apparent in a woman poet's affirmation of a tradition to which most women's poetry never officially belongs.

3 Strategies of storytelling

The facts of being largely excluded from the canon of literature and of being misrepresented within it do not, of course, mean that literary and poetic tradition does not matter to women poets. It is important not only as the context of poetic meaning, which determines how particular texts can be read, but also, more simply, as the subject matter of poems. The ways in which women poets use the material of myth and storytelling occupy the rest of this chapter.

European myth and fairytale fascinate women poets to the point of obsession. Poems by women which retell myths include H.D.'s classic *Trilogy* (1944) and *Helen in Egypt* (1961); Margaret Atwood's 'Circe / Mud' sequence (*Selected Poems*, 1974); Judith Kazantzis's *The Wicked Queen* (1980), which uses classical and Christian legends as starting points for feminist narratives; and Michelene Wandor's *Gardens of Eden* (1984), which ingeniously dramatizes female subjectivities by relating Jewish mythology, on the one hand, through Lilith's perception of Bible stories, and on the other, Eve's European tour of classical legends. Fairytale material is also the subject of many poems by Stevie Smith, of Anne Sexton's *Transformations* (1972) and Liz Lochhead's *The Grimm Sisters* (1981), all discussed below (pp. 43–56). The current interest, among British feminists particularly, in recasting such material is apparent from the large number of poems in the anthology *One Foot on the Mountain* (1979) which link autobiographical anecdote with legends or fairy-stories,[29] as Olga Broumas does in *Beginning with O* (1977), to alter the meaning of the myths.

Broadly speaking, the world of fairy-stories seems to attract those poets whose idiom is closest to ordinary speech, whereas poets interested in classical mythology often combine this with modernist formal experiment, as H.D. did. Two difficult but brilliant texts of French feminist *écriture*, both discussed below in Chapter 5 (pp. 153–8), adopt similar strategies: Monique Wittig's *Le Corps lesbien* (1973), which turns most of the figures of Greek myth into women (Zeyna, Ulyssea, Achillea, etc.),[30] and Luce Irigaray's *Speculum* (1974), which recasts the myth of Plato's Cave as a womb-and-birth fantasy.[31] Nor is this interest confined to poets: many women novelists,[32] expecially those influenced by feminism, have re-worked myths or legends into their fiction.

Feminist critics who have written about the way women poets use and revise myths and fairytales have stressed the connections between myth and subjectivity:[33] 'Myth belongs to "high culture" and is handed "down" through the ages by religious, literary and educational authority. At the same time it is quintessentially intimate material, the stuff of dream life, forbidden desire, inexplicable motivation.'[34] Certainly it is the awareness, derived from the insights of psychoanalysis and anthropology, of myth as representing and defining human consciousness, that has made it so attractive to poets; it is not accident that the revival of myth in poetry post-dates the appearance of *The Interpretation of Dreams* and *The Golden Bough*. But what defines a myth as such is not only its status as a repository of meaning, but something simpler if more recalcitrant: it is a narrative (oh dear yes, a myth tells a story). Coincidentally, Liddell and Scott's *Greek–English Lexicon* defines the root meaning of *mythos* as 'anything delivered by word of mouth, speech',[35] and despite its antiquity, myth always has a close connection with speech, since it is after all a form of storytelling.

The connections between direct speech, traditional legend, and the experience which that legend both depends on and defines, have been clarified by the critic Walter Benjamin in the classic essay on Leskov, 'The Storyteller' (1936). Benjamin interprets storytelling as, essentially, the communication of experience: 'Experience which passes from mouth to mouth is the source from which all storytellers have drawn . . . Every real story . . . contains, openly or covertly, something useful. The usefulness may, in one case, consist of a moral; in another, some practical advice; in the third, a maxim. In every case the storyteller is a man [*sic*] who has counsel for his hearers.'[36] Storytelling, Benjamin argues, is a dying art because in the present (i.e. for him the 1930s), human experience is less and less explicable in ordinary terms: 'never has experience been contradicted more thoroughly than strategic experience by tactical warfare, economic experience by inflation, bodily experience by mechanical warfare, moral experience by those in power'.[37] Storytelling, a distilled, concentrated art associated with the artisanal mode of production in which direct speech between individuals is the norm of communication, has been superseded by mass-produced information and explanation. 'No event comes to us without being already shot through with explanation . . . [whereas] it is half the art of storytelling to keep a story free of explanation as one reproduces it.'[38] Information comes to us as disposable knowledge, instantly forgettable: 'the value of information does not survive the moment when it was new'.[39] Stories, by contrast, remain in the memory by virtue of 'that chaste compactness which precludes psychological analysis'.[40] The ideal condition for storytelling is a room full of people engaged in tedious, repetitive manual labour. 'Boredom is the dream bird which hatches the egg of experience. A rustling in the leaves drives him away. His nesting places – the activities that are intimately associated with boredom – are already extinct in the cities and declining in the countryside.'[41]

Women are conspicuously excluded from Benjamin's essay on storytelling; his typical storyteller is either a master craftsman or a sailor,[42] and even the dream bird in his allegory is a broody cock. Yet his arguments apply readily enough to the experiences and traditional occupations of women, a point made in Liz Lochhead's poem 'The Storyteller', which reads like a feminist gloss on his essay:

> No one could say the stories were useless
> for as the tongue clacked

five or forty fingers stitched
corn was grated from the husk
patchwork was pieced
or the darning done.

. . . .

To tell the stories was her work.
It was like spinning
gathering thin air to the singlest strongest
thread. Night in
she'd have us waiting held /
breath, for the ending we knew by heart.[43]

It is also possible for the feminist critic to extend
Benjamin's suggested connection between storytelling and
communicable experience to the poetry that has come out
of feminism. Direct speech and storytelling are, after all,
characteristic activities in the women's movement, an
important aspect of feminist politics being the insistence
we place on the importance of women articulating their
own experiences, breaking a stifling or barren silence by
telling their own authentic stories. Our articulation of
subjective experience produces the unpublished narratives
of consciousness-raising groups. The rise of storytelling
poetry among women poets, especially feminists, is very
likely to be connected with the existence of a feeling –
and a practice – of community between women. On the
other hand, Benjamin's arguments cannot simply be
transferred into a feminist milieu, for it is clear that the
'experience' which his storyteller communicates is different
from the personal histories told in a C-R group, and
different again from a feminist poetry of experience based
on the axiom that 'the personal is the political'. The
'counsel' in the folktale is a matter of maxims and
generalities – a proverbial collective wisdom which has
become obsolete in the era of late capitalism; likewise,
there is a similarity, not an identity, between the small-

scale political communities of feminists and the pre-industrial villages where 'true storytelling' originated. Yet Benjamin's essay remains illuminating to feminists, particularly his remarks on the fairy-story as told to children, the only form in which traditional storytelling is still alive. 'The first true storyteller is, and will continue to be, the teller of fairytales. Whenever good counsel was at a premium, the fairytale had it, and where the need was greatest, its aid was nearest ... The wisest thing, so the fairytale taught children in olden times and teaches them to this day, is to meet the forces of the mythical world with cunning and with high spirits.'[44] Fairy-stories do *not*, however, hold out the same 'good counsel' for both sexes, their heroines being notoriously less remarkable for 'cunning and high spirits' than for the naive passivity which characterizes Snow White, Red Riding Hood and the Sleeping Beauty. Yet if women poets invoke the fairytale in order to counter its proverbial 'experience' with their own axioms, how are they to avoid those 'explanations' which kill the memorable simplicity and wisdom of true storytelling? This question cannot be answered *a priori*, but only through examining particular instances of storytelling poets; it is now time to look at some detailed examples.

4 Stevie Smith and other storytellers

Stevie Smith has remarkable assets as a storytelling poet: a narrative gift, an original imagination, an easy relation to tradition, and as Hermione Lee says, a flexible, serious and witty 'talking voice'.[45] She is of course a prose writer as well, but as a storyteller she seems to me at her best in her poems, exploiting their conciseness and using different line lengths to control cadences with remarkable skill. She is a highly allusive writer; besides her habitual references to fairy-stories, hymns and nursery rhymes (all popular forms), she has 'a strong attachment to the English tradition ... a powerful feeling for Greek and French classical tragedy, for Virgil, Homer, Catullus, Plotinus and Seneca, for the liturgy and the Book of Common Prayer'.[46] This literary sophistication, combined with her easy, allusive, conversational style, might suggest that her poems are little more than musical manifestations of the English weakness for cultivated family jokes. Seamus Heaney hints as much when he writes, characterizing her 'memorable voice' shrewdly but with a discernible trace of Irish distaste, 'It is essential to bring to an appreciation of these poems an ear aware of the longueurs and acerbities, the nuanced understatements of educated middle-class English speech.'[47] But if Stevie Smith's qualities were limited to conversational wit, literary sophistication, and a deceptively casual way with free verse, she would hardly qualify as a storyteller. Her poems are 'light verse' in the sense defined by Auden: that is, verse which implies a community of shared assumptions between poet and audience, without the poet being either its spokesman or a Romantic seer whose insight and imagination necessarily surpass those of his or her listeners. Light verse can be and often is serious, the nature and degree of its seriousness being determined by what assumptions the poet and audience have in common.

Auden's definition of light verse has an obvious likeness to Benjamin's contemporary conception of the storyteller (his Introduction to the *Oxford Book of Light Verse*, which explains his use of the term, post-dates 'The Storyteller' by only two years).[48] Each man is trying to understand and rescue from critical oblivion a generally ignored popular genre; though Auden's notion is much the looser, since it applies to verse produced by and for any homogeneous social group. And Stevie Smith's verse corresponds to both definitions: popular for a long time with readers rather than critics, her work has both the easiness of light verse and the simplicity and strangeness of storytelling as Benjamin defines it. When she brings a well-known fable or fairytale into a poem, instead of 'explaining' it, she tells it with the voice of someone inside the story. It is up to the reader or listener to decide what the moral is:

> The story is familiar
> Everybody knows it well
> But do other people feel as nervous
> As I do? The stories do not tell
>
> Ask if they will be happier
> When the changes come
> As already they are fairly happy
> In a frog's doom?[49]

Similarly, the poems in which a heroine or hero departs into some 'altogether elsewhere' are left to speak for themselves:

My darling grew pale he was responsible
He said we should go back it was reasonable
But I wished to stay with the angel in the dark wood at
   night.

My darling said goodbye and rode off angrily
And suddenly I rode after him and came to a cornfield
Where had my darling gone and where was the angel now
The wind bent the corn and drew it along the ground
And the corn said, Do not go alone in the dark wood.
Then the wind drew more strongly and the black clouds
   covered the moon
And I rode into the dark wood at night.

. . . .

Loved I once my darling? I love him not now.
Had I a mother once? She lies far away.
A sister, a loving heart? My aunt a noble lady?
All all are silent in the dark wood at night.[50]

Stevie Smith's finest story is in a poem which is not a revision of fairytale archetypes at all: 'Angel Boley', a poem which was obviously sparked off by the 'Moors Murders', first appearing in 1966[51] shortly after Ian Brady and Myra Hindley were convicted of torturing and murdering several children. But the words of the opening, for all their geographical detail, are distanced into a comparatively remote past:

> There was a wicked woman called Malady Festing
> Who lived with her son-in-law, Hark Boley,
> And her daughter, Angel,
> In a house on the high moorlands
> Of the West Riding of Yorkshire
> In the middle of the last century.

When Angel overhears her mother saying to Hark 'It is time / to take another couple of children into our kitchen', the poem shifts to a moment of melodrama ('Hark laughed, for he too was wicked') and then to a style of sophisticated description:

> But Angel who was not happy and so
> Lived out her life in a dream of absentmindedness
> In order not to be too much aware
> Of her horrible relatives, and what it was
> That happened every now and then
> In the kitchen; and why the children who came
> Were never seen again, this time
> Came out of her absentmindedness and paid attention.
> I know now, she said, and all the time I have known
> What I did not want to know, that they kill all
>   the children
> They lure to this house.

Unlike Hark and Malady, whose characters are simply defined by their roles in the story, being wicked, arrogant and stupid enough to despise the household drudge, Angel is doomed to complexity and conflict. She is an ordinary person who finds that, against her will, she is living in the morality-play which her name evokes. As she faces the truth, her speech is direct and powerful:

> Angel wandered into the woods and she said, No
>   more children
> Are going to be murdered, and before they are
>   murdered, tormented
> And corrupted; no more children are going to be
>   the victims
> Of Mother Lure and my husband, Hark. Dark was
>   the look then
> On Angel's face, and she said: I am the Angel of
>   Death.

The climax of this speech, and the turning point of the poem, is Angel's assumption of responsibility in the words that will forever after define her identity: 'I am the Angel of Death.' Her passionate simplicity then changes to the narrator's more educated style for the details of the horrible family's domestic arrangements (Angel is their despised cook-housekeeper), and her tactics:

> As soon as Angel
> Said to herself, I am the Angel of Death
> She became at once very practical and went out into
>   the woods and fields
> And gathered some A. Phalloides, commonly called
>   the 'white' or deadly
> Amanita, an inedible mushroom of high toxicity.
>   These poisonous fungi
> She put into a soup, and this soup she gave
> To Hark, and her mother Malady, so that they
>   died.

This prosaic style points up the fact that once Angel's decision is taken, nothing matters but practicalities; hence the poet's reproduction of textbook language. (Her details are, incidentally, accurate: the common name of the fungi Angel uses is the Death Cap, of which there is a pure white variant called the Destroying Angel.)[52] But the story does not end here. Angel gives herself up as a murderer to the police, explaining why she could not have got rid of Hark and Malady in the same way (no evidence) in a rather wordy passage which is the poem's only weak spot. (True, it establishes that there really was no way out of Angel's dilemma, but this could have been taken as read anyhow.) After this Angel never speaks except to say: ' "I am the Angel of Death", / So they put her in a lunatic asylum, and soon she died.' This death is fitting, not because she is a murderess (the poem is not really about people getting their just deserts) but because once she has taken on herself the destiny of being the 'Angel of Death', her own life is ended. She becomes a local heroine and the occasion of an ambiguous miracle: the villagers write on her tombstone, 'She did evil that good might come', and when these words are erased by order of the vicar, they reappear.

> And no man came to write on the tombstone
> The forbidden words. Yet when morning came
> Again the words were on the tombstone.
> So the Vicar said, It is the hand of the Lord.

> And now in that graveyard, at that grave's head
>   between the yew trees
> Still stands today the tombstone of Angel with the
>   words writ on it,
> 'She did evil that good might come.' May God
>   be merciful.

The prayer for mercy in the beautifully cadenced last line seems to be for Angel, who has done what is theologically forbidden, and may mean no more than than she needs forgiveness. But we have been left in no doubt that her action stopped an obvious evil in the only possible way, and if we agree that she did right in becoming the 'Angel of Death', she deserves pity and admiration; her much more wicked victims need forgiveness more than she does. The meaning of the prayer would then be 'May God be merciful because people can't afford to be,' but the poet refuses to say whether Angel is right or wrong. It is the absence of commentary which makes her story so haunting; as Benjamin says, it is half the storyteller's art *not* to explain and to leave the audience to discover for themselves the story's 'counsel' – which in this particular instance has a distinctly feminist edge. For though the poem's horrors are obvious and even melodramatic, its real drama is to be found in the dilemma of the apparently powerless girl, confined in a subordinate domesticity, who 'never knew, / Or wanted to know, what was going on around her', who wakes up to the knowledge that her home is a place of evil, to ignore which is to collude with it, and that she alone is responsible for stopping it. But the price of action is to be defined by her tragic dilemma; once she has become the 'Angel of Death', there is nothing else for her to be.

Although even 'Angel Boley', with its explanations of Angel's wilful absentmindedness, does not entirely conform to Benjamin's conception of narrative simplicity, Stevie Smith's overall success as a storyteller comes from the way she tells her often complicated tales without analysing their significance. The other storytelling poets whose work I discuss in the rest of this chapter are less oblique and more straightforwardly interpretative. First, Anne Sexton's *Transformations* (1972), consisting of sixteen stories retold from Grimm, is as its name suggests a work of revision. This is not, as with Stevie Smith, a matter of shifting the emphasis of the story so that the result is an entirely new plot; it derives solely from the poet's reinterpretation of the stories, which as Suzanne Juhasz says 'begin with present-day situations of which the stories are archetypes'.[53] The voices in the poems are therefore all contemporary, and the narrator, 'a middle-aged witch, me',[54] speaks as a witty, sardonic American:

> No matter what life you lead
> the virgin is a lovely number:
> cheeks as fragile as cigarette paper,
> arms and legs made of Limoges,
> lips like Vin Du Rhône,
> rolling her china-blue eyes
> open and shut.
> Open to say
> Good Day Mama
> and shut for the thrust
> of the unicorn.[55]

The pungent ironies of *Tranformations* are based on the insights (and the dogmas) of psychoanalysis. One of the best, 'Rumpelstiltskin' is about the mutilated daemonic libido:

> I am the enemy within.
> I am the boss of your dreams.
> No. I am not the law in your mind,
> the grandfather of watchfulness.
> I am the law of your members,
> the kindred of blackness and impulse ...
> and no child will ever call me Papa.

Most of Anne Sexton's reinterpretations turn the Grimm stories into the gruesome versions of an Oedipal family drama, mostly as experienced by daughters. It is like a much less cosy poetic anticipation of Bettelheim's *The Uses of Enchantment* (which twice quotes poems from *Transformations* to illustrate its psychological readings of fairytales).[56] Her heroines, sleek naive virgins, are at the mercy of evil witches or puritanically loving fathers — somewhat too loving in the case of Briar Rose (Sleeping Beauty), the victim of

the nightly horror
my father thick upon me
like some sleeping jellyfish.[57]

In these poems, the only relationship between an older and a younger woman that is not hostile is the doomed idyll of Mother Gothel and Rapunzel:

We are two clouds
glistening in the bottle glass.
We are two birds
washing in the same mirror.
We were fair game
but we have kept out of the cesspool.
We are strong.
We are the good ones.
Do not discover us
for we lie together all in green
like pond weeds.
Hold me, my young dear, hold me.

. . . .

They are as tender as bog-moss.
They play mother-me-do
all day.
A woman
who loves a woman
is forever young.[58]

Into this game of 'mother-me-do' enters the prince, unattractive but with the trump card of a 'dancing stick'. He and Rapunzel live happily ever after, 'proving that mother-me-do / can be outgrown / like fish on Fridays'; Mother Gothel is left to pining and dreams. This orthodox Freudianism has, it is true, the potential to be read differently as a radical lesbian fable; this is done by Olga Broumas in a version of 'Rapunzel' which is

patently a re-vision of Anne Sexton's poem. Broumas
takes Anne Sexton's method of applying the fable to real-
life situations, which in her case are autobiographical.
The result is here defiant erotica, in which the original
story exists only as a reference-point:

> Climb
> though my hair, climb in
> to me, love
>
> hover here like a mother's wish
> You might have been, though you're not
> my mother. You let like hair, like static
> her stilled wish, relentless
> in me and constant as
> tropical growth.[59]

But there is an ironic ambiguiity in the lines Olga
Broumas quotes from Anne Sexton's poem: 'a woman /
who loves a woman / is forever young.' Though Mother
Gothel has all the lyricism, the poem defines her
lovemaking as the childish game 'mother-me-do'; its
make-believe innocence is doomed by heterosexual
maturity. It is a depressing fable for lesbian feminists.

In fact, the tendency of the revisionary storytelling in
Transformations is remarkably determinist. The critic
Alicia Ostriker, making very high claims for its 'revisionary
mythmaking', writes of Anne Sexton's storyteller: 'She
emits an air of exhilarating mental and emotional liberty,
precisely because she is distanced from the material she so
penetratingly understands ... Philosophically, the axis
Transformations turns on is Necessity (here seen as fixed
and damaging psychosocial patterns) versus Freedom.'[60]
But if the power of these stories really does derive from
their correspondence with unconscious mental processes,
or even only with 'fixed and damaging psychosocial
patterns', then no commentary, however penetrating, can
of itself abolish their power. Identifying the processes that

govern you, with whatever amount of wit and irony, does not mean freedom from them. The alleged remoteness of the storyteller from the archetypes she relates, resembles T.S. Eliot's epigrammatic snub to iconoclasts: 'Someone said, "The dead writers are remote from us because we *know* so much more than they did." Precisely, and they are that which we know.'[61] In *Transformations*, knowledge is bounded by the Oedipal drama which is 'that which we know'.

A conscious feminism affects Liz Lochhead's *The Grimm Sisters* (1981) and Judith Kazantzis's *The Wicked Queen* (1980) in a way not shared by Anne Sexton or Stevie Smith. Judith Kazantzis's poems include reinterpreted incidents from classic texts ('Portia's Lover gets the right answer'), a sequence devoted to character types called the 'Seven Deadly Sins', and retellings of classical legends like 'Clytemnestra', which is first told by the poet and then by the heroine:

Clytemnestra, queen of the grand absurd name,
Clytie in her nightie
the big bosom pushing through frills
as she drowns the hero in his bath

. . . .

Iphigenia my daughter, sits on my lap
in the evening, talking.
I brush her black hair and kiss her shoulders,
she wriggles and smiles, don't do that
kisses me with a soft mouth
as when a baby she kissed my breasts . . .
Over the years after, at Mycenae
I saw you, graveless
your ashes fed to Poseidon
small handful of my daughter
plump and twelve years old
whose body they burned.

This is powerful because it evokes Clytemnestra's love
for her sacrificed daughter, *not* as a psychological
interpretation of the story but simply as a dramatic
experience. In a different but related way, Liz Lochhead
uses motifs from fairy-story as allegories of female
experience, metaphors for an already realized drama.
Thus, in 'The Last Supper', an about-to-be-jilted woman
is preparing a final evening:

> Already she was imagining it done with, this feast,
>   and exactly
> what kind of leftover hash she'd make of it
> among friends, when it was just
> The Girls . . .
> Yes, there they'd be, cackling round the cauldron,
> spitting out the gristlier bits
> of his giblets;
> gnawing on the knucklebone of some
> intricate irony;
> getting grave and dainty at the
> petit-gout mouthfuls of reported speech;
> 'That's rich!' they'd splutter
> munching the lies fat and sizzling as sausages.

In other poems Liz Lochhead plays around with plots
from Grimm, amalgamating 'Rapunzel' and 'Rumpelstiltskin' with a dash of the Sphinx legend to articulate a
woman's exasperation at male obtuseness: ' "I love you?"
he came up with / as finally she tore herself in two.' Or
she interweaves traditional fable with ironic commentary,
not unlike a Scottish Anne Sexton:

> And if, as the story goes
> nine times out of ten
> He took you by the milkwhite hand & by the
>   grassgreen sleeve
> & laid you on the bonnie back & asked of you
>   no leave,

well, so what?
You're not the first to fall for it,
good green girdle and all –
with your schooltie rolled in your pocket
trying to look eighteen. I know,
All perfectly forgiveable.
Relax.[62]

Although this particular poem has a fairly positive ending ('what about you? / How do you think Tam Lin will take / all the changes you go through?'),[63] even Liz Lochhead does not escape the determinist implications of interpretative storytelling.

For revisionary storytelling is, unless the poet makes her traditional material into a new plot altogether, a limited project. All the poems I have discussed here have vitality, poignancy and wit (though except for Stevie Smith's, they often sound better in summary than they do when read right through), but they neither exorcize nor assume the power of their originals. Their virtue is wit rather than haunting simplicity, which cannot survive their sophisticated interpretations of the fairytales they relate – though again Stevie Smith is a partial exception. I do not mean by this that the storytelling poems are failures, only that their success is necessarily limited.

The nature of that limitation clarifies women's difficult relationship to literary tradition, which needs some recapitulation here. As I have argued above, to belong to this as reader and writer, and not to belong as a woman, is an uncomfortable paradox, which the images of the woman writer's lonely struggle, produced by the feminist critics Adrienne Rich, Sandra Gilbert and Susan Gubar, represent as a personal dilemma for the poet. But not all women poets may feel it as such, and in any case the problem of tradition lies as much in the context of association which defines and modifies the meaning of particular poems, as in the emotional obstacles with which traditional misrepresentations of Woman confront the poet. To assert that there is no problem, because as readers and writers we do inherit tradition, means ignoring the exclusion and misrepresentation of women on which that tradition is based (and often goes along with assenting to a conventional division between the wide range of men and the narrow occupations of women).

The recasting of myth by women poets looks like a solution to these paradoxes. For the appeal of such traditional material as myth and fairy-story, especially for feminists, lies not only in its archaic prestige, but in its strong connections with human subjectivity, so that using this material seems to be a way of at once escaping the constrictive hierarchies of tradition and gaining access to the power of definition. Alicia Ostriker sees such 'revisionary mythmaking' as a project to raid 'the sanctuaries of existing language, the treasuries where our meanings of "male" and "female" have been preserved'.[64] But just because this material is both traditional and powerful, it is resistant to recasting. Political interpretations can deflect but not alter its meanings, which either return to haunt the poem that overtly discards them, or vanish into witty analysis. Strategies of storytelling are not, finally, effective in overcoming the paradoxes of exclusion. There is truth as well as optimism in the claim that women need to make their own tradition.

CHAPTER 3

TOWARDS A WOMAN'S TRADITION

1 Female traditions: models and criticisms

Although masculine literary and poetic traditions are pervasive, as I argued at length in the preceding chapter, it is difficult for women poets either to insert themselves into this tradition, or to appropriate its materials for their own use, since these prove extremely opaque to the light of female, let alone feminist definition. The idea of an alternative women's tradition is obviously attractive, since it offers a way out of the poetic (and critical) dilemma faced by women of inheriting conventions and definitions which deny us authority. The idea of a woman's tradition would enable feminists not only to rewrite our independent history of women poets, but to construct a context of poetic meaning in which women's poems were not constantly overdetermined or undermined by patriarchal suggestion and symbol; finally, it would work more generally to help make a woman's discourse thinkable. All of these make the (re)creation of a woman's tradition into an ambition well worth pursuing, even though the very magnitude and importance of the project make it problematic and controversial.

The notion of a woman's tradition has been propounded recently by different critics in three main versions. First is the model offered by Sandra Gilbert and Susan Gubar in *The Madwoman in the Attic*, symbolized by their exemplary critical fable of the woman writer's inner struggle between her conformist self (i.e. the good daughter of patriarchy) and her alter ego, the creative Wicked Queen. Their version of women's tradition (summarized and argued with at length above in pp. 28–31 of Chapter 2) posits this as oppositional, not independent; they have a more elaborate and sophisticated version of the usual radical feminist emphasis on women's experience of oppression as the authenticating touchstone of women' writing, since for them the significant experience of the woman writer is her mental conflict between collusion with and rebellion against the patriarchal culture in which she lives and against which she pits her imaginative struggle. For these critics, articulating the rebellious, dangerous self (in whatever concealed or distorted forms) is the essence of women's writing.

A similar emphasis on women's writing their own experience is found in Adrienne Rich's beguiling and influential version of a woman's tradition. Rich has not worked this into a book-length study; it is first sketched in her essay 'When We Dead Awaken: Written as re-vision',[1] and is indicated or assumed in later essays and poems. The defining experience of the woman writer is for Rich not her solitary mental conflict with the bogeys of patriarchy, but her consciousness of solidarity, of an identity shared with other women. This is indicated in the memorable fable Rich invents in 'When We Dead Awaken' to exemplify the woman writer's problems with masculine tradition: when the young woman's search for 'guides, maps, possibilities'[2] turns up only the alienating image of Woman as imagined by men, Rich's suggested solution is, naturally enough, that she should read the work of other women: 'So what does she do? What did I do? I read the older women poets with their peculiar keenness and ambivalence: Sappho, Christina Rossetti, Emily Dickinson, Elinor Wylie, Millay, H.D.'[3] Turning to other women means liberating her own identity: the latter part of Rich's autobiographical essay tells how she gradually freed herself from her evasive habit of using masculine or androgynous poetic forms to avoid confronting her own deepest thought, finally becoming able to write these directly instead of obliquely.[4]

Rich's fable of the woman writer finding herself through her links with other women is marvellously suggestive and evidently contains much truth. But as a model for a woman's tradition, it has a problem shared by Gilbert and Gubar's 'madwoman', namely that in directing attention to the female self behind or within the poems, it tends to subsume all *particular* histories into the representative fable. For however necessary it may be to think in terms of 'the woman poet' or 'the woman writer' in the early stages of constructing feminist criticism, she is entirely mythical; she doesn't exist in real life, any more than 'the archetypal male poet' does. What does exist is an immense variety of women poets, often divided by major differences of class, race and circumstances, and writing in a multiplicity of discourses; and any account of a woman's tradition has to take account of these differences and separations. It is arguable that the necessary task for feminists is not re-creating a 'woman's tradition', but asking 'in *which* tradition, feminine and otherwise, do particular writers belong?'

On the other hand, to insist on the multiplicity of discourses engaged in by women writers is to risk letting what is specifically female drop out of the argument. What is valuable in Rich's fable of the woman poet's quest for self-expression and her version of woman's tradition is not only that these vividly dramatize a problem and its solution; it is also her insistence that women's poetry needs to be read differently from men's, and in its own terms; not because it calls for indulgence, but because it changes poetic possibilities. Her listing of the women poets she herself read, which helps to make a new context of meaning for her own poems, is an indication of the kind of different reading which women's poetry calls for. What Rich always emphasizes is the network of influence between women, the links between past and present poets, between the 'foremothers' from whom we inherited our thoughts and ourselves as daughters aware of our inheritance.[5] This image of the community of women is as apparent in Rich's poetry as in her essays: *The Dream of a Common Language* (1978) and *A Wild Patience Has Taken Me This Far* (1981) are full of poems which memorialize female communities and the women of the past, an emphasis substantiated in *A Wild Patience* by two pages of bibliographical notes which make available to other women the history Rich both draws on and re-creates in the poems. Rich's implied model of a woman's tradition is similar to that of Ellen Moers in *Literary Women* (1978), where Moers both traces lines of influence between women writers and refers her interpretations of particular texts to the writer's experience of childbirth (as with Mary Shelley's *Frankenstein*) or infantile eroticism (as with Christina Rossetti's 'Goblin Market'),[6] but a crucial difference between these critics is that, unlike Moers, Rich holds that female psychology is essentially lesbian. In her analysis, the experience of relating to one's poetic mothers, and thus discovering one's own capacity for self-expression in poetry, parallels for the lesbian poet her own experience, through her sexuality, of readmission to her primordial infantile bond with her mother. I think there are problems with this assumption that the woman's tradition is the articulation of woman-centred experience (briefly, that this defines woman's discourse much too narrowly), but will return to this later.

A quite different model of a woman's tradition, less well known than either Rich's or Gilbert and Gubar's, is offered by the critic Margaret Homans in *Women Writers and Poetic Identity* (1980). Her argument is not addressed to the writer's psychology but is made through an examination of the 'masks' – that is, positions within post-Romantic poetic discourse – from which it is possible for women poets to speak. She argues that Romantic transcendence, especially as achieved and theorized by Wordsworth, is a compelling and even necessary ideal for the poet, but one impossible for woman to achieve; partly because Romantic subjectivity claimed to represent all humanity but in fact privileged the masculine gender (cf. my own Chapter 1, pp. 8–11), but more importantly because Wordsworthian transcendence assimilated the feminine to Mother Nature, so that Woman in his poems typically ends up like Lucy, brute matter whose final destiny is to be alienated from the consciousness that mourns her:

> No motion has she now, no force,
> She neither hears nor sees,
> Roll'd round in earth's diurnal course
> With rocks and stones and trees.[7]

Margaret Homans's book examines how three Romantic women writers negotiated these problems: Dorothy Wordsworth the diarist, who was almost completely blocked as a poet; Emily Brontë, partially successful in her poems but only achieving the real breakthrough in *Wuthering Heights*; and finally Emily Dickinson, who created a truly great and original poetry by exploiting the duplicity of language through a series of fictional masks. She argues that the ambition of feminist poets like Adrienne Rich to 'rename the world' is essentially an (unconscious) revival of the Romantic myth of the transcendent poet as Adam giving names to the creatures of his vision; she is, correspondingly, hostile to the prevalent notion that the work of the woman poet consists in transcribing raw (or only lightly cooked) experience. The appropriate figure for women poets to model themselves on, she suggests, is Eve in *Paradise Lost*, for precisely because of her association with falsehood she is 'the first speaker of a non-literal discourse . . . To become poets, women must shift from seeing themselves as daughters of nature and as parts of a world of objects to seeing themselves as daughters of an Eve reclaimed for poetry.'[8] Her idea of a 'feminine tradition'[9] is thus at the opposite pole from Rich's idea of a woman's tradition as a linked network of female self-expression.

It will be apparent from these summaries that I have disagreements with all these versions of a woman's tradition, with the exception of Margaret Homans's – but I think it is arguable that what she is exploring is not so much a woman's tradition as a strategy whereby women poets can negotiate their reaction to an otherwise alien and debilitating (for them) poetic discourse, namely Romantic transcendence. Because both the 'Madwoman' version of woman's tradition and Adrienne Rich's idea of a network of female identities emphasize women's subjective awareness of themselves, both theories share the risk of overemphasizing rather narrow versions of female experience as the authenticating basis of the traditions they imagine. As I have suggested in a previous chapter, 'experience' is an attractive but finally unhelpful criterion for women's poetry, not only for formalist reasons (see Chapter 1, pp. 5–7) which would anyway be inapplicable to the general question of a female discourse, but because of its potential reductiveness – or, to put it differently, its essentialism. This term, current in French feminist thought and among critics influenced by it, means the assumption – whether overt or only implied – of an authenticating 'essence' of female subjectivity, usually identified with female bodily experience, which includes and defines all women.[10] The point of this term, when used as a criticism, is that to think of female subjectivity as an absolute category in itself is to obscure the actual history of individuals, both in the microcosmic sense of the family dramas and fantasies whereby sexual identity is acquired, and in the much larger sense of the institutions, politics and discourses that (partially) determine our lives. Rich's idea of the 'primary presence of women to each other'[11] as the bedrock of female psychology – and therefore of poetry too (psychology being in her analysis the basis of poetry) – is, I think, essentialist in this sense.

All of these problems arise from the difficulty – not insuperable, but not deniable either – of matching the self-evidently feminist notion of a woman's tradition with the possibly non-feminist material produced by women poets. This is not just an abstract issue; several articulate women have voiced their unease about the essentialist orthodoxy implied by the idea of a woman's tradition authenticated by female experience. For example, the critic and novelist A.S. Byatt, when asked in an interview what she thinks about the idea of a woman's tradition as posited in Moers's *Literary Women*, replies:

> What frightens me about a critic like Moers is that I'm going to have my interest in literature taken away by women who see literature as a source of interest in women . . . I'm interested in women anyway. My interest in literature has always been my way out, my escape from the limits of being female.[12]

This is actually unfair to Moers, who was not at all a reductive critic, but A.S. Byatt's point is not in itself negligible. When women writers are read from the unexamined assumption that what makes them important is their femaleness, the results can be as inappropriate as she suggests, like for example this remark from an interview with another woman novelist, Esther Broner:

> I didn't understand Willa Cather, why she had to speak through a man, through the archbishop. What happened to her? She was a lesbian, she made all her intense commitments to women.[13]

This speaker finds Willa Cather's obliqueness puzzling and unacceptable because of her own ahistorical notions of feminism and sexual identity. Similar assumptions surface in Adrienne Rich's more nuanced reproach for the same writer:

> And Willa who could not tell
> her own story as it was
> left us her stern and delicate
> respect for the lives she loved —[14]

Though this characterizes Willa Cather's art admirably, it still leaves one wondering why the poet apparently thinks that the artist *ought* to have told 'her own story as it was'. Although A.S. Byatt is perhaps overreacting in being 'frightened' by such literal-minded application of the idea of a woman's tradition, her response is understandable:

> Everywhere it has been snowing on the dead,
> look how the glittering cover has been spread
> over the blackened complicated dead.[15]

Anachronistic notions of the essential identity of female psychology seem to me just such a 'glittering cover' imposed on the historical realities of actual women writers. On the other hand, it would be downright perverse to argue from these occasional crudities that the project of reconstructing a woman's tradition is itself obscurantist, since it is largely thanks to the women engaged in that work that women poets and novelists (like Willa Cather herself)[16] have been disinterred from critical and publishing oblivion.[17] What emerges from these arguments is the difficulty of making a woman's tradition workable as a critical construct without either oversimplifying its components or losing sight of what is specific to women.

2 The question of bad poetry

Another difficulty raised by the idea of a woman's tradition is that of establishing the grounds on which poetry is valued as well as understood. A.S. Byatt's perfectly legitimate argument that she does not want to be read only because of her femininity has a converse complement in the suspicion sometimes voiced in literary journals, that feminists overvalue bad or mediocre work simply because it is written by women. Often enough, this takes the crude form of a kneejerk reaction to feminist challenging of literary authority, which is found in complaints that feminists 'won't let us enjoy Kingsley Amis' – in other words, apparently bland expressions of personal preference thinly disguising demands that feminists endorse them. There is, nevertheless, a genuine problem in 'placing' bad or mediocre poetry by women (which certainly exists) in the context of a woman's tradition. Feminist critics often argue – rightly – that conventional scholarship and criticism has, because of its masculine bias, either ignored classic texts by women or so misread them as to obscure most of their meaning. The literary histories of the 1930s, discussed above in Chapter 1 (pp. 20–5) are an instance of just such neglect of women. But it has to be admitted that sometimes the 'buried treasure' does turn out to be just old iron. A case in point is the women's poetry of the First World War which was revived and anthologized in Catherine Reilly's *Scars Upon My Heart* (1981). However grateful we are to the editor for disinterring these poems (which are full of interests to the social historian of ideologies), it cannot be pretended that many of them are good, most being uncomfortably reminiscent of the 'original contributions' section of an old-fashioned school magazine. In other words, the general effect is conventional, sincere and amateurish.[18]

The unsatisfactoriness of this poetry is apparent in

Vera Brittain's line, from which the anthology's title and epigraph are taken: 'Your battle wounds are scars upon my heart.'[19] Because 'heart' is a metonym for 'self', and because 'scars' connote healing as well as injury, Brittain evokes not only the trauma on her memory, but also the possibility of its fading, and thus suggests, damagingly, the experiential gap between his bodily suffering and her pity; this of course undermines the poet's declared identification with the injured man. For the words of a poem to contradict its overt sense need not necessarily be damaging, but it becomes so when the irony is unintentional. And the line is technically amateurish as well; in order to make the clumsy internal rhyme and broken scansion of '*are scars* upon my *heart*' (my italics) sound right, you have to artifically de-stress what should be a long vowel, so that it reads 'your battle-wounds're scars'. What makes the poignancy of both this line and the whole poem it occurs in, is its tragic historic context, and especially the death in battle of the brother it addresses, four days after the poem was written.[20]

The women poets included in *Scars Upon My Heart* are, bafflingly perhaps for the feminist critic, soaked in the English poetic tradition represented by Palgrave's *Golden Treasury* and Quiller-Couch's *Oxford Book of English Verse*. The allusions to Milton, Shelley, Keats, Wordsworth and Housman which Paul Fussell in *The Great War and Modern Memory* has shown at work in the soldiers' poems[21] are to found here, and so are the same Georgian poetic motifs of dawn, dusk, birdsong and flowers, especially roses.[22] Such indebtedness is not in itself an obstacle to achievement. The traditional approach can be seen at its best in one of the few truly successful poems in the anthology, Eleanor Farjeon's 'Easter Monday: in memoriam E.T.' (presumably the poet Edward Thomas). This negotiates the gap between the soldier's unapproachable experience of death and the woman's experience of bereavement through an unobtrusive use of traditional motifs. The poem has the length (fourteen lines) and the organized concision of a sonnet, but not its rhyme-scheme. It needs quoting in full to make its effects plain:

> In the last letter that I had from France
> You thanked me for the silver Easter egg
> Which I had hidden in the box of apples
> You liked to munch beyond all other fruit.
> You found the egg the Monday before Easter
> And said, 'I will praise Easter Monday now —
> It was such a lovely morning.' Then you spoke
> Of the coming battle and said 'This is the eve.
> Goodbye. And may I have a letter soon.'
>
> That Easter Monday was a day for praise,
> It was such a lovely morning. In our garden
> We sowed our earliest seeds, and in the orchard
> The apple-bud was ripe. It was the eve.
> There are three letters that you will not get.[23]

This is a 'dead letter' which can never reach its recipient; hence, ironically, the conversational ease of the poem's opening. The echoing of the dead man's words emphasizes what he and the poet shared; a delight in life cut off with the brief 'There are three letters that you will not get.' The irony is pointed up by the word-play of the deceptively casual opening: 'In the *last* letter' (my italics). The poem's poignancy also derives from its beauty of detail and phrasing; 'The apple-bud was ripe' combines loving sensuous observation with associations of promise and fruition (the bud's reddish colour, the blossom about to open and the 'earliest seeds'); there are also at work the traditional associations of morning with youth and hope, while the ominously rapid 'It was the eve' suggests the life truncated. There is a buried but detectable reminiscence here of Shakespeare's Sonnet 33: 'Full many a glorious morning have I seen ... Anon permit the basest clouds to ride / With ugly rack on his celestial face,' while the way the ripe apple-bud represents and communicates delight in creation, recalls the strength and delicacy of Edward Thomas's own nature poetry. These traditional associations of morning, Easter, seeds and buds with growth and promise are discernible but not obvious; the details retain the literal status which the poem's conversational letter-form gives them, just as the Miltonic phrase 'beyond all other fruit' is hardly noticeable beside the obvious colloquialism of 'You liked to munch'. Equally unobtrusively, the irony implied by sending letters to a dead man articulates the greater contradiction of the untimely death that destroys the continuities on which the poem's relation with tradition depends.

But even this fine poem is limited by the constraints of its traditional blank verse form. Its compassion and irony are finely achieved, but do not quite have the intensity of Enid Bagnold's little-known contemporary prose work, *A Diary Without Dates* (1919), which is remarkable not only for the quality of its witness but for its 'poetic' way of making the spaces tell as much as the words:

> It was the first time I had heard a man sing at his dressing. I was standing over by the sterilizer when Rees's song began to mount over the screen that hid him from me. ('Whatever is that?' 'Rees's tubes going in.')
>
> It was like this: 'Ah . . . ee . . . oo, Sister!' and again 'Sister . . .'
>
> I heard her voice. 'Now then Rees, I don't call that much of a song.' She called me over to make his bed and I saw that his left ear was full of tears.
>
> When one shoots at a wooden figure it makes a hole. When one shoots at a man it makes a hole, and the doctor must make seven more.[24]

Such combinations of intensity and detachment are not, however, characteristic of the poets in *Scars Upon My*

Heart, the majority of whom draw fairly straightforwardly on patriotic ideologies and Romantic poetic convention, often handling both very naively. Judith Kazantzis's honest and sympathetic introductory essay, acknowledging this problem, treats the poems mainly as evidence for the ways in which middle-class women (which all these poets were) experienced the war as (with some exceptions) patriotic non-combatants. I would say, more harshly, that the poems are valuable to the social historian precisely because of their often uncritical handling of War, Sacrifice, Poetry and Religion: there is no professional finish to disguise thought and feeling.

If most of the women poets of *Scars Upon My Heart* demonstrably failed to transcend the chauvinist ideologies and literary clichés of their time, does this also mean that they failed to produce a significant woman's discourse? 'Certainly not' is one influential answer. Sandra Gilbert has argued in two recent articles[25] a persuasive, though to me not wholly convincing, case for reading the poetry and prose of Englishwomen during the Great War as evidence that women's notorious patriotic bloodthirstiness and ready acceptance of the wartime sacrifice of their menfolk actually manifested rage against their male oppressors.[26] The Great War, Gilbert suggests, at least temporarily dispossessed male citizens of the patriarchal primacy that had always been their birthright. In this context, women's enthusiasm for war manifested their desire for freedom from masculine coercion, their pleasure at partly getting it, and their vicarious revenge on the dominant sex (not so vicarious, either, in the case of men shamed into joining the army by women distributing white feathers for cowardice to men not in uniform). Yet to emphasize women's power in a society in which they could not even vote seems like stretching subjective perceptions – and even fantasies – too far. The wartime strength of women must have seemed greater than it was, partly because of the contrast with the previous years when women's labour was less needed and their presence less felt or acknowledged, and partly because of the imagined association between the patriotic myth of the Motherland (not to mention the dissenting writers' version of this: one's country as the old sow that eats her farrow)[27] and the power of women through our emotional influence. It is certainly true that this association, and its accompanying fantasies, were and are very powerful. For example, in the passage from Enid Bagnold's *Diary Without Dates* quoted above, the Sister (who is not responsible for inflicting Rees's horrible wound) nevertheless appears as both more powerful and more guilty than she can actually have been – an impression which the final sentence about the holes which the *doctor* must make does not wholly efface. And yet, overall, Sandra Gilbert's emphasis on female power and rage means underplaying the ideologies and conventions with which these women writers are profoundly engaged, in favour of an essentialist emphasis on female anger as the motor and explanation of all women's writing.

The critical dilemma which emerges from considering the ideologically fascinating but aesthetically dubious is, however, more apparent than real. We do not in fact have to choose between the Scylla of historical determinism (seeing women as the victims of social and literary conventions and ideologies) and the Charybdis of essentialism (seeing all women's writing as determined by our suppressed energies). The fact that women are deeply engaged with masculine traditions and discourses, sometimes (though not always) to the detriment of their writing, should not be a problem for critics who would theorize a woman's tradition, unless this tradition is imagined as unrealistically autonomous. It is actually important that a woman's tradition be seen in relation to patriarchal discourse, so long as the relation is understood as opposition.

3 Sexual politics and lesbian strategies

The poets who have done most to imagine and to create a woman's tradition, and whose work I discuss in the rest of this chapter, are a group of American lesbian feminists: Olga Broumas, Judy Grahn, Irena Klepfisz, Joan Larkin, Audre Lorde and Adrienne Rich. All of these speak from an overtly political standpoint, their work deriving much of its energy and direction from the lesbian feminist critique of human experience; and they are consciously creating a new tradition, not depending on an old one. In the essay introducing *Lesbian Poetry* (1981, ed. Elly Bulkin and Joan Larkin, in which all these poets appear), the editors insist that lesbian poetry be recognized as intensely political and as breaking new ground, arguing that their own editorial work contributes to the (re)discovery of a lesbian tradition, ending an imprisoning silence. They contend that for lesbian poets, the lack of their own history is a major stumbling block, a problem associated with the exclusion from literary discourse and publication of texts by black and working-class people; they are thoroughly hostile to 'traditional (white bourgeois male) values relating to every facet of poetry – its style, its structure, its subject, its audience'.[28] Lesbian poetry in this account is at once marginal to its own culture and central to America's deepest concerns. 'These lesbian poets were outsiders in American society. They felt no stake in its traditions, in its establishments, in its social/political/aesthetic values. Instead they sought to create a tradition that was anti-literary, anti-traditional, anti-hierarchical.'[29] This subversive tradition both derives from and validates an understanding of lesbian existence as the vital, revolutionary core of feminism. The editors describe their own work as the latest in a series of self-assertions by lesbian poets, whose tradition they define very broadly, quoting Louise Bernikow:

Whether all the woman-to-woman relationships that existed in the lives of these poets were explicitly sexual or not is difficult to know, for taboo was always in the way and evidence that might have told the true nature of these relationships is missing. Yet what matters most is not who did what to whom in bed, but the direction of emotional attention. Mostly, then, these women turned to women – and understanding that might be the beginning and end of a non-patriarchal biography.[30]

In this analysis, sexual practice is seen as less important then loyalty and love between women: a position close to that taken by Adrienne Rich in the well-known pamphlet *Compulsory Heterosexuality and Lesbian Existence* arguing for the notion of the 'lesbian continuum' to describe all positive relationships between women:

> I mean the term . . . to include a range – through each woman's life and throughout history – of women-identified experience; not simply the fact that a woman has had or has consciously desired genital sexual experience with another woman. If we expand it to include many more forms of primary intensity between women, including the sharing of a rich inner life, the bonding against male tyranny, the giving and receiving of practical political support . . . we begin to grasp breadths of female history and psychology which have lain out of reach as a consequence of limited, mostly clinical definitions of 'lesbianism.'[31]

For these poets, correspondingly, lesbian commitment is a form of political practice. Obviously, these arguments are not immune to criticism. The new 'anti-traditional, anti-establishment poetry' that Elly Bulkin and Joan Larkin argue for has a distinctly Whitmanesque tone: the solitary man sounding his barbaric yawp being replaced by a collective of woman-identified women speaking their visions to each other, while Adrienne Rich's claim that lesbian feminism represents a primordial female authenticity replicated in all woman-identified relationships is a piece of thoroughly monolithic essentialism. But it is not necessary to assent to all these arguments and assertions (I doubt if all the poets I am discussing would agree with Rich on the 'lesbian continuum', for instance), only to understand them as constituting the political and intellectual context of the poetry. For these women poets, it is as important to be lesbian as to be feminist. And lesbian-feminist politics are directly connected with the vitality, energy, and especially the range of Audre Lorde, Joan Larkin and their peers. Their consciousness of themselves as outside 'normal life' makes for intellectually and morally ambitious achievement, and their work is the crystallization of their efforts to understand and criticize, and change that normality. In their different ways they make their subject nothing less than a total critique of the American world they inhabit, for as Sheila Shulman writes in 'Hard Words', lesbians are 'more human because necessarily / more conscious'.[32]

A literal-minded reader might expect such a commitment to sexual politics to produce two kinds of poem: on the one hand, overt polemic, and, on the other, love poetry articulating lesbian sexual experience. Certainly, both of these exist. Lesbian poets have produced powerful polemics; they are particularly strong on memorializing the violence and injustice endured by obscure or forgotten people, as in Judy Grahn's 'A Woman Is Talking to Death':

> death sits on my doorstep
> cleaning his revolver
>
> death cripples my feet and sends me out
> to wait for the bus alone,
> then comes by driving a taxi

> the woman on our block with 6 young children
> has the most vacant of eyes
> death sits in her bedroom, loading
> his revolver[33]

Audre Lorde is even more direct in 'Power':

> The policeman who shot down a 10-year-old in Queens
> stood over the boy with his cop shoes in childish blood
> and a voice said 'Die you little motherfucker' and
> there are tapes to prove that. At his trial
> the policeman said in his own defense
> 'I didn't notice the size or nothing
> only the color' and
> there are tapes to prove that too.[34]

In this context it is maybe misleading to oppose political to love-poetry. Judy Grahn insists on this in 'A Woman Is Talking to Death' when she tells how she refused to stay in a dangerous place to witness to someone's innocence:

> I'm afraid, he said, stay with me, be
> my witness – 'No,' I said, 'I'll be your
> witness – later', and I took his name
> and number, 'but I can't stay with you,
> I'm too frightened of the bridge, besides
> I have a woman waiting
> and no licence –
> and no tail lights –'
> So I left –
> as I have left so many of my lovers.[35]

The effect of this long poem when read in its entirety is to redefine 'love' so as to mean not only eroticism but political commitment and the loyalty of the dispossessed to one another. But poems that articulate lesbian sexuality also occur in the work of these women, as in Rich's evocation of the way adult and infantile sexual experience interweave in

the homesickness for a woman, for ourselves
for that acute joy her head and arms
cast on a wall, her heavy or slender
thighs on which we lay, flesh against flesh,
eyes steady on the face of love; smell of her milk,
   her sweat,
terror of her disappearance, all fused in this hunger[36]

Joan Larkin's 'Some Unsaid Things' is also powerfully erotic:

> I was not going to say
> how you lay with me
>
> nor where your hands went
> & left their light impressions
>
> nor whose face was white
> as a splash of moonlight
>
> nor who spilled the wine
> nor whose blood stained the sheet
>
> nor which one of us wept
> to set the dark bed rocking
>
> . . . .
>
> nor what confusion came
> of our twin names
>
> nor will I say whose body
> opened, sucked, whispered
>
> like the ocean, unbalancing
> what had seemed a safe position[37]

Similar marine imagery crops up in the work of the best-known lesbian poet of the erotic, Olga Broumas, such as 'Amazon Twins':

> more than the head
> is crustacean-like. Marine
> eyes, marine
> odors. Everything live
> (tongue, clitoris, lip and lip)
> swells in its moist shell. I remember the light
>
> warped around our bodies finally
> crusted, striated with sweat.[38]

Or Broumas deciphers the significance of parts of the body:

> I work
> in silver the tongue-like forms
> that curve around a threat
>
> an arm-pit, the upper
> thigh, whose significance stirs in me
> like a curviform alphabet
> that defies
>
> decoding, appears
> to consist of vowels, beginning with O, the O-
> mega, horse-shoe, cave of sound.[39]

But with the exception of Olga Broumas's work, erotic poems are not too frequent in the writing of these lesbian poets; they occur mainly as parts of long poems like Irena Klepfisz's 'From the Monkey House' or Judy Grahn's 'She Who'. All of this lesbian poetry is powerful, moving and exciting; it is so direct and offers such intense vicarious experience that the reader may (despite the profusion of metaphor in the erotic poems) have the illusion that this poetry *is* reality.

Yet, all this being said, the work I have surveyed so far does not in itself seem to constitute an alternative tradition, except in terms of the subject matter of the poems. 'In terms of subject matter' is of course a major qualification; what makes lesbian poetry so invigorating is the ambitiousness of its practitioners and their willingness to tackle major issues. But subject matter of itself does not make up a poem, much less a tradition; this latter is evoked much more obliquely by these poets, in the form of myth.

4 Towards the lost matriarchies: Audre Lorde and Judy Grahn

> She Who floods like a river and
> like a river continues
> She Who continues
>
> (Judy Grahn)[40]

> What is now thought was once only imagin'd.
> (William Blake)[41]

For lesbian feminists constructing a woman's tradition, the past is not primarily a matter of literary history. If these women invoke masculine traditions at all, it is only to define themselves by opposition. The past world which Audre Lorde, Judy Grahn and Adrienne Rich create in their poems through reference, allusion and – occasionally – direct description, is that of a buried but still persisting female culture reaching back to pre-patriarchal civilizations. This is the positive, mythical side of these women's refusal of the patriarchal order in which they exist: they create a world of female experience where women's power and knowledge are taken for granted – power meaning not domination but fullness and intensity of being. Poetry is the ideal vehicle for this mythical world, because as Adrienne Rich writes, 'poetry is above all a concentration of the power of language'.[42]

But these poems are not theoretical treatises or literal histories; still less are they credos. (The only poets I know of who have worked out theories of Goddess-worshipping matriarchy, including a theology of the Goddess and a history of her overthrow, are Robert Graves and Robert Bly,[43] neither of them, obviously, being lesbian feminists.) These women poets are not proposing a system of belief but suggesting a mythology through fragmentary details, references and allusions. A partial exception is Adrienne Rich, who does devote a chapter in *Of Woman Born* to a critical but sympathetic discussion of theories of matriarchy, but even she treats the evidence mainly as a source for numinous imagery. And different poets work this mythology in different ways: for example, the Dahomey poems in Audre Lorde's *The Black Unicorn* evoke the women of an alien society, with their customs and beliefs, as a valid alternative to the world of hostile, racist and sexist America, whereas Judy Grahn's long poems *She Who* and *Queen of Wands* celebrate women's power to create and endure without representing any female society at all; instead she stylizes aspects of women's experience into fables. The significance of all these poems often lies in the relation they evoke between a mythical past available only to the imagination and an all too intrusive hostile present:

I want our own earth   not the satellites, our

world as it is   if not as it might be
then as it is: male domination, gangrape,
    lynching, pogrom
the Mohawk wraiths in their tracts of leafless birch
watching[44]

It becomes possible, then, for a woman who feels herself an exile in her own country to rediscover a homeland through the representation of an authentic female realm. This mythology carries a number of related significations. It may represent:

(1) an uncolonized, unexploited, unviolated realm of escape from patriarchy's ruinous present, or
(2) a means of imagining communities of women living, working and producing a specifically female culture, or
(3) a form of utopia in which feminist ideals and values can exist as norms instead of marginal alternatives, or
(4) a source of numinous female imagery, or
(5) a celebration of the power of women in which biological capacities such as childbirth or menstruation symbolize life-principles, or
(6) a means of evoking qualities of mind (such as intuition) and modes of relationship (such as mutual support) between women which exist under patriarchy, but only under pressure of taboo or discouragement.

This list is not meant as a thematic schematization of all matriarchal motifs; obviously, meanings which I have separated to indicate different possible emphases do in practice overlap, as with 2-3 and 4-5. In practice, individual poems evoke some or all of these meanings at once. For example, Audre Lorde often uses numinous female imagery in her poems to articulate dissent, as in this extract from '125th Street and Abomey':

> Head bent, walking through snow
> I see you Seboulisa
> printed inside the back of my head
> like marks of the newly wrapped akai
> that kept my sleep fruitful in Dahomey
> and I poured on the red earth in your home
> those ancient parts of me
> most precious and least needed
> my well-guarded past
> the energy-eating secrets

> I surrender to you as libation
> mother, illuminate my offering
> of old victories
> over men over women over my selves
>
> . . . .
>
> give me the woman strength
> in this cold season[45]

Here the poet invokes the goddess Seboulisa, 'The Mother of us all', and a primordial female culture to exorcize the fears and to counter the dangers of the winter city. Where she writes directly about the female principle, there is less tenderness apparent than power, as in 'From the house of Yemanja' (the goddess of oceans):[46]

> I bear two women on my back
> one dark and rich and hidden
> in the ivory hungers of the other
> mother
> pale as a witch
> yet steady and familiar
> brings me bread and terror
> in my sleep
> her breasts are huge exciting anchors
> in the midnight storm
>
> All this has been
> before
> in my mother's bed
> time has no sense
> I have no brothers
> and my sisters are cruel[47]

These are images of power, though not imagined as material domination but as potency:

> The Coniagui women
> wear their flesh like war
> bear children who have eight days
> to choose their mothers
> it is up to the children
> who must decide to stay
> on the third day
> they creep up to her cooking pot
> bubbling over the evening's fire
> and she feeds them
> yam soup
> and silence[48]

This is a powerfully imagined fragment of a world which is complex, assured and utterly alien to the arid, embittering world of contemporary America, 'between the smoking ruins of a black neighbourhood in Los Angeles / and the bloody morning streets of child-killing New York'.[49]

It is a poetic power similar to this that Adrienne Rich praises in her preface to Judy Grahn, 'as if forces we can lay claim to in no other way became present to us in sensuous form'.[50] Power in this sense means fullness and intensity of being; it is only indirectly a political idea. In fact, Judy Grahn's overtly political energies are engaged not by the fantasy of ruling but by the experience of powerlessness. 'A Woman Is Talking to Death' is partly about the responsibilities that victims and exiles have towards each other, while the 'Common Woman Poems' celebrate the ability of oppressed and marginal women to survive against all the odds. These poems, full of narrative particularities, indicate that for Judy Grahn the imaginable social world is the American present. This is borne out by one of her prose statements: 'One characteristic of workingclass writing is that we often pile up many events within a small amount of space rather than detailing the many implications of one or two

events. This means both that our lives are chock full of
action, and that we are bursting with stories that haven't
been printed, made into novels, dictionaries, philos-
ophies.'[51] The 'She Who' poems by contrast celebrate
women's power to create, to endure and to sustain, but
not by telling real-life stories:

> She Who molds her blood in a bowl
> in a bowl, in a bowl of blood
> and the bowl, and the bowl and the blood
> and the foam and the bowl, and the bowl
> and the blood belong to She Who holds it.
>
> She shook it till it got some shape.
> She shook it the first season and lost some teeth
> She shook it the second season and lost some bone
> She shook it the third season and some body was born.
> She Who.[52]

This is not a literal creation myth, but a consciously
mythical way of understanding the creation of new life.
Similarly, relationships between women appear in the
'She Who' poems in stylized forms, so that grief for 'my
first lover and longtime friend' becomes a plainsong 'for
ritual use':

> want of my want, i am your lust
> wave of my wave, i am your crest
> earth of my earth, i am your crust
> may of my may, i am your must,
> kind of my kind, i am your best[53]

Or affection is stylized into the runic 'Carol and':

> Carol and her
> hack saw
> well worn
> torn back
> bad spine
> never-mind

> timberline
> clear mind
> Carol and her
> hard glance
> stiff dance
> clean pants
> bad ass
> lumberjack's
> wood axe[54]

The way Judy Grahn condenses qualities, experiences and ideas into memorable fables is particularly apparent when she writes of the problem for a lesbian feminist of writing about women's beauty without fetishizing it. This is the theme of the parable of the 'most blonde woman' who chooses to throw off her skin and become 'a bald woman / with bleeding pores' loved by

> small hard-bodied spiders
> with dark eyes and an excellent
> knowledge of weaving.
> They spun her blood into long strands
> and altogether wove millions of red
> webs, webs red in the afternoon run.
> 'Now', she said, 'Now I am expertly loved,
> and now I am beautiful.'[55]

Judy Grahn's poems do not represent any historical matriarchy, even by allusion; she saves the particularities of women's lives for poems about present-day America. (This is true at least of her earlier work. The myth-based poems in *Queen of Wands* (1982) combine narrative particularity with a free form, in my view much less successfully.) The 'She Who' poems are of any time and no time, since She Who has always existed:

> I am the wall at the lip of the water
> I am the rock that refused to be battered

I am the dyke in the matter, the other
I am the wall with the womanly swagger[56]

Powerful and exciting as this poetry is, the deployment
of myths of matriarchy or the Goddess is obviously liable
to certain criticisms. Because the existence of prehistoric
matriarchies has not been proven, accepting the idea
means taking speculation as fact; and this particular
speculation, after all, originated with nineteenth-century
anthropologists whose idea of a primitive society based
on 'mother-right' was, as Rosalind Coward has shown in
Patriarchal Precedents, profoundly influenced by imperi-
alist myths of the 'childhood of the race'.[57] It is hard to
dispute Dorothy Dinnerstein's contention that 'the main
significance of these myths is psychological, not historical
. . . and this question has more active societal importance
for the light that thinking about it sheds on our fantasy
life than for the light that its definitive answer might shed
upon our actual history'.[58] In other words, it is the kind
of notion that tells less about the thing it is supposed to
explain than about the person who believes it. And there
is something worrying in all these poems about the
opposition implied between a bedrock female nature on
the one hand, persisting through and in spite of
patriarchal culture on the other. This is paradoxically
similar to D.H. Lawrence's ideas of 'blood-consciousness':
womb and vulva symbolism get privileged instead of the
phallus, and his Etruscans are replaced by the women of
Dahomey, but the basic notions of eternal sexual
principles are very similar.

But the force of these objections is much diminished by
the fact that none of the poems which deploy the imagery
of reference of the 'lost matriarchy' should be taken
literally. The poets are not enforcing an orthodoxy but
suggesting a mythology. 'She Who' and the women of
Dahomey are by no means escapist fictions: the poetry
which they energize includes both an oppositional
critique of contemporary society and an imagined alterna-

tive to it. Although I do not wholly agree with the terms in which these alternative female worlds are put, the feminist mythology seems to me not (as the Dinnerstein quotation might suggest) an indulged fantasy but an important way of imagining – and therefore creating – the possibility of a woman-centred discourse.

5 Communities of women: Adrienne Rich and Irena Klepfisz

Could you imagine a world of women only,
the interviewer asked. *Can you imagine*

a world where women are absent. (He believed
he was joking.)   (Adrienne Rich)[59]

The work of creating a woman-centred discourse in poetry is not only a matter of imagining lost matriarchies. Equally important is the effort to rethink history in predominantly female terms, retrieving from oblivion not a lost matriarchy but a community of women, a project which informs the poetry of Adrienne Rich, who from the outset has been deeply engaged with the ideas of history and of poetic tradition (though her conception of these has altered radically). Rich continually emphasizes our distance from and only partial knowledge of the past: a knowledge which her poetic and critical practice seeks to retrieve and extend, as she writes in 'Diving into the Wreck':

> I came to explore the wreck.
> The words are purposes.
> The words are maps.
> I came to see the damage that was done
> and the treasures that prevail.[60]

The past represented by 'the drowned face always staring / toward the sun'[61] is not only the poet's alter ego but collective history. Rich has since moved on from commemorating anonymities to evoking an increasingly individualized female past. The poems in *The Dream of a Common Language* contemplate the lives of past and present women, sometimes unnamed because they never achieve identity, as with the blocked writer of 'To a Poet', 'where language floats and spins / *abortion* in / the bowl',[62] or because they are unknown, like the forgotten communities of women in 'Natural Resources' who co-operate to make the necessities of life. Other poems, however, celebrate known heroines like Marie Curie, Elvira Shatayev and Paula Becker,[63] while the theme of the retrieval of history is pointed up in the following collection, *A Wild Patience Has Taken Me This Far*, by the addition of source notes which also remind readers of the feminist scholarship which has made the poems possible.

Adrienne Rich is a poet of brilliant fragmentary particularities; the intensity of her poems derives as much from their discontinuities as from their passages of vivid intelligibility. Reading them involves deciphering and interpreting their gaps: a demand that works very well in her meditations on the fragmentary relics of vanished lives in 'From An Old House in America':

Other lives were lived here
mostly un-articulate

yet someone left her creamy signature
in the trail of rusticated

narcissus straggling up
through meadowgrass and vetch

. . . .

Like turning through the contents of a drawer:
these rusty screws, this empty vial

> useless, this box of watercolour paints
> dried to insolubility –
>
> but this –
> this pack of cards with no card missing
>
> still playable
> and three good fuses
>
> and this toy: a little truck
> scarred red, yet all its wheels still turn[64]

Here Rich creates a poetry of relics whose significance surfaces through the poet's effort to understand them. Details like broken toys, or, in 'Natural Resources', 'shoehorns / of german silver, a gilt-edged book / that opens into a picture-frame- / a biscuit-tin of the thirties'[65] are enumerated by a mind to which they are 'at once remote and familiar';[66] that is, a poet who, like an archaeologist, labels her finds as a first step to reconstructing in imagination the lives of those who used them. Rich's genius for vivid fragments has, I surmise, been assisted by her reading in the poetry of H.D., especially *Trilogy*: the free-verse couplets and the mode of presenting junkshop rubbish recall the meditative opening of 'The Walls Do Not Fall' where bombed houses are seen as Egyptian tombs opened up by investigators:

> . . . we pass on
>
> to another cellar, to another sliced wall
> where poor utensils show
> like rare objects in a museum[67]

The mystery of the 'poor utensils' commemorated in Rich's poems is increased by the irony that such junkshop trivia, being the only evidence of vanished lives, has to represent also the vast abstractions: death, loss and distance. The poet knows that the past cannot be reached; yet in the imaginative attempt to comprehend the lives of women like the one who 'left her creamy signature / in the trail of rusticated / narcissus', the community of women gains a tenuous existence in the imaginations of poet and reader.

Many of the poems in *A Wild Patience* enact such an imaginative reconstruction of communities of women. 'Culture and Anarchy', for example, ends with a triumphant assertion of identity between past and present:

> Late afternoon: long silence.
> Your notes of yellow foolscap drift on the table
> while you go down the garden to pick chard
> while the strength is in the leaves
> crimson stems veining upwards into green.
> How you have given back to me
> my dream of a common language
> my solitude of self.
> I slice the beetroots to the core,
> each one contains a different landscape
> of bloodlight filaments, distinct rose-purple
> striations like the oldest
> strata of a southwest canyon
> an undiscovered planet laid open in the lens
>
> > *I should miss you more than any other*
> > *being from this earth . . .*
> > *Yes, our work is one.*
> > *we are one in aim and sympathy*
> > *and we should be together*[68]

Though the quotation is italicized and separated on the page, the link between the poet's solitary meditations and the letter from Elizabeth Cady Stanton to Susan B. Anthony is so plainly the analogy between the lives of these Victorian friends and the experience of Rich and her lover that the poem reads as an assertion of lesbian identity across the discontinuity of time, while the domestic details of the gathering and slicing of beetroots connote in complex ways a realm of experience and vision. The celebration of the poet's everyday productive happiness and of the traditional 'woman's world' of undervalued domestic tasks is obvious, but more important is the contemplative consciousness that sees the beauty of 'the crimson stems veining upwards into green' and associates their colour with the rock of the Arizona canyons (inhabited by the lost pre-Columbian civilizations), so that the beets' 'rose-purple / striations' become metonyms of an essential female bedrock, their crimson vulval circles being miniature representations of the planet's 'core' laid open to the lens of the poet's vision – a geological metaphor that enables Rich to define a sexualized female universe that persists throughout human history:

> the stone foundation, rockshelf further
> forming underneath everything that grows.[69]

Yet this red rock is a thoroughly essentialist metaphor of identity, from which all the lived differences of women's experiences and choices have disappeared: instead of a community of women, we have a symbol of femaleness. Much stronger is the sequence 'Turning the Wheel', also in *A Wild Patience*, where the poet imagines lives and experiences that are not her own - that is, the vanished world of the Hohokan Indians. Here Rich stresses unbridgeable dislocation as against the desire to grasp an alien being in one's own, inevitably oversimplifying terms:

> if she is the famous potter
> whose name confers honor on certain vessels
> if she is wrist-deep in mud and shawled with dust
> and wholly anonymous
> look at her closely if you dare

> do not assume that you know those cheekbones
> or those eyesockets, or that still-bristling hair.[70]

One hardly notices here that the poet has had it both ways, actually seeming to abolish the gap between modern consciousness and archaic woman by insisting that it be acknowledged. The demonstrative adjectives in '*those* cheekbones / or *those* eyesockets' evoke the vision of a staring face whose alien particularity is so vivid as to blind one to the fact that this 'desert witch' is after all an apparition produced by the words of the poet and no less a fiction than the reducing of woman to a symbol, against which the immediately preceding poem warns us ('so long as she merely symbolises power / she is kept helpless and conventional').[71] The poem certainly works, but as a powerful illusion; it is, I think, finally less successful than her archaeologically orientated poems which contemplate the relics of alien lives with a shock of recognition, as in 'Burden Baskets':

> But, behind glass, these baskets
> woven for the young women's puberty dances
> still performed among the still surviving
> Apache people; filled with offerings:
> cans of diet Pepsi, peanut brittle,
> Cracker Jack, Hershey bars
> piled there, behind glass, without notation
> in the anthropologist's typewritten text[72]

Rich's notation of such surprising fragments firmly establishes the differences, as well as the similarities, between the lives of women in different cultures; and this is a much-needed corrective to the possible essentialism implied in the myth of a timeless female world. But where myth is evoked, the danger always exists of taking it literally; and in any case, this is not the only means available to poets of making both the community of women and specificity of female experience thinkable in their own terms.

An alternative strategy, dealing much more directly with history, is taken by the Jewish lesbian poet, Irena Klepfisz. It is true that she has produced highly figurative poems, as in 'Poems from the Monkey-House', but this sequence, as its title suggests, dramatizes its own fictionality. Other poems are rooted in history rather than myth, and her long prose poem 'Bashert' is a passionate and successful effort not only to imagine but to work out the meaning of the destruction of the European Jews – which is also her own family history. Because 'Bashert' is so tightly structured, each paragraph redefining the last, it is necessary to quote at length to give the feel of the poem. This extract is from part 2, 'Chicago 1964':

I am walking home alone at midnight. The university seems an island ungrounded. Most of its surrounding streets have been emptied. On some, all evidence of previous life removed except for occasional fringes of rubble that reveal vague outlines that hint at things that were. On others, old buildings still stand, though these are hollow like caves, once of use and then abandoned. Everything is poised. Everything is waiting for the emptiness to close in on itself, for the emptiness to be filled up, for the emptiness to be swallowed and forgotten.

Walking home, I am only dimly aware of the meaning of this strange void through which I pass. I am even less aware of the dangers for someone like me, a woman walking home alone at midnight. I am totally preoccupied with another time, another place. Night after night, protected by the darkness, I think only of Elza who is dead. I am trying to place a fact about her, a fact which stubbornly resists classification: nothing

that happened to her afterwards mattered. All that
agonized effort. All that caring. *None of that mattered!*

At the end of the war friends come to claim her. With
the calculated cunning of an adult, the eight year old
vehemently denies who she is. No, she is not who they
think. Not a Jew. They have made a mistake. Mixed
her up with another Elza. This one belongs here, with
her mother.

She is simply being scrupulous in following her parents'
instructions. 'Do not ever admit to anyone who you
are. It is our secret. Eventually we will come for you.
Remember! *Never admit who you are!* Promise![73]

But after the war, Elza's parents have died in a
concentration camp. She is adopted by Americans, and
has an apparently successful life. But 'None of that
matter[s]': she is tormented by restless misery and kills
herself at the age of twenty-five.

A story she once told me remains alive. During the war,
the Polish woman sends her to buy a notebook for
school. She is given the wrong change and points it out.
The shopkeeper eyes her sharply: 'Very accurate. Just
like a Jew. Perhaps you are a little Jewess?' And Elza
feels afraid, and wonders if the woman sees the truth in
her blue eyes.[74]

The poem now returns to the 'present' of the student
walking through Chicago, meditating on Elza's death:
'Are there moments in history which cannot be escaped
or transcended, but which act like time warps permanently
trapping all those who are touched by them? And that
which should have happened in Poland in 1944 and
didn't, mustn't it happen now? In 1964? In Chicago? Or
can history be tricked and cheated?'[75] The poet stands in

the almost-demolished street, seeing in it a significance for herself:

> I see the rubble of this unbombed landscape, see that the city, like the rest of this alien country, is not simply a geographic place, but a time zone, an era in which I, by my very presence in it, am rooted. No one simply passes through. History keeps unfolding and demanding a response. A life obliterated around me of those I barely noticed. A life unmarked, unrecorded. A silent migration. Relocation. Common rubble in the streets.
>
> I see now the present dangers, the dangers of the void, of the American hollowness in which I walk calmly day and night as I continue my life. I begin to see the incessant grinding down of lives for stamps, for jobs, for a bed to sleep in, of death stretched imperceptibly over a lifetime. I begin to understand the ingenuity of it. The invisibility. The Holocaust without smoke.
>
> Everything is poised. Everything is waiting for the emptiness to be filled up, for the filling-up that can never replace, that can only take over. Like time itself. Or history.[76]

Irena Klepfisz draws one so successfully into her visions of lives destroyed like Elza's, or damaged like those of Chicago's dispossessed, that it is easy not to notice that all the people in her poem are women. Our attention is drawn to their tragedy and endurance, not to their gender; and her strength comes partly from her awareness (manifested in other poems as well) of the multiple oppressions endured by slumdwellers, including the obliteration of their history, as well as the horror of the European holocaust. (Her awareness of history both as chronicle and as the events which escape chronicling, is crucial here.) Yet her poems do not, as all this might suggest, work as ammunition for a humanist critique of their feminism; '*Bashert*' and other poems in *Keeper of Accounts* do not insist on their feminist significance, but this is apparent nonetheless in the way that the poet simply takes for granted that the lives and experiences of women are important.

A comparison of '*Bashert*' with Carol Rumens's recent moving poem 'Outside Oswiecim' clarifies the way feminism works in the former poem. The two poets voice a similar impotence of grief in the face of the genocide of the Jews; there is a likeness of tone as well as meaning between Irena Klepfisz's 'None of that mattered!' and Carol Rumens's 'How is it possible I can make no difference?'[77] But unlike '*Bashert*', Carol Rumens's poem is, as its title implies, written 'outside' the experience it commemorates: 'spoken' by a series of voices (the poet, the victims, even the fascists), it dramatizes its distance from its own material. In her essay on Carol Rumens, Anne Stevenson praises 'Outside Oswiecim' for a sympathy whose detachment transcends the poet's own gender, and which is intimately bound up with her awareness of the ironic fictionality of her chosen form – as when she insists that it is not generalities but minute particulars which she must retrieve from oblivion:

Emblem, exhibit, witness – Husserl's suitcase
flanked the rust-brown pile. The cold twine of its handle
I touch, then grasp for a faceless, weightless stanza.[78]

The obvious difference between the poems is that unlike 'Outside Oswiecim', '*Bashert*' is explicitly written out of personal experience, part of its theme being the poet's acceptance of the painful inheritance of her own Jewishness and her personal involvement with the Holocaust (she and her mother survived and escaped to America), both of which had merely bored and embarrassed her as an American teenager. As readers, we follow the experience of the poet who announces at the end, weighing every word, 'Yes. It is true. I am a keeper of accounts',[79] and who has worked through the painful confrontation with the past which is implied in accepting with her Jewish as well as her female identity the feminist axiom that the personal is political. But the difference is not only that one is writing from within the tragedy, the other from outside it. It is in itself a trivial matter that Carol Rumens mentions only one victim by name – that is, a distinguished man, Husserl, whereas Irena Klepfisz mentions her friend 'Elza' and an unnamed woman who helps her mother to survive a famine, but it marks an important difference of emphasis. So does her acknowledgment of the dangers disregarded by her obsessed younger self as she walks the midnight streets alone. These feminist emphases are, however unobtrusively made, central to the meaning of 'Bashert', and are the means whereby the poet, in a very different way from those who evoke a lost matriarchy via the mythology of the Goddess, reconstructs a community of women in history, which is at the same time a version of feminist poetry of experience at its strongest. It seems likely that it is the poet's participation in a community of lesbian feminist writers that helps to make this interweave of poetry and history possible – from which it follows that the community of women exists not only as invoked in poems, but in the present.

The most coherent and satisfying version of a woman's tradition, then, is the reconstruction through poems of women's past, whether actual as in 'Bashert' or semi-mythical as in Audre Lorde's Dahomey poems, Judy Grahn's 'She Who' sequence, or Adrienne Rich's evocations of American history. Conversely, it emerged from the early part of this chapter that as a critical construct, the notion of a woman's tradition is difficult because it seems to demand that women's poetry be conceived purely in its own terms. This demand proves unrealistic, partly because of its implied essentialism, partly because when women's poems are closely examined, it usually appears that women poets are engaged with patriarchal tradition, if only by way of opposing it. A woman's tradition and a woman's discourse are still in the process of construction, an effort which is inseparable from feminist commitment in the here and now.

CHAPTER 4

TWO-WAY MIRRORS: PSYCHOANALYSIS AND THE LOVE-SONNET

The Mistress to her Lover

The word I say is not the word I mean.
You listen, speak, explain and analyse –
The air is empty where our speech has been.

Your tongue explores the salty and the clean
Savouring our complexity of lies;
The word we say is not the word I mean.

Gesture and tone, the spoken and the seen,
The mouth affirming what its smile denies –
The air is empty where our speech has been.

I touch you and your skin enjoys the keen
Outlines of pleasure which my hands incise.
The word you say is not the word I mean.

My patterns move across your sense's screen,
I watch myself in your possessing eyes.
The air is empty where our speech has been.

What truth I am is nameless and unseen.
The language of my silence signifies
The word I say is not the word I mean.
The air is empty where our speech has been.[1]

1 Imaginary identities in the love-poem

The love-poem as it appears in the Western tradition of poetry represented by Petrarch and Sidney is characteristically spoken by a male poet celebrating the beauty and virtue of an unattainable woman who is at once the object of his desire, the cause of his poetry and the mirror which defines his identity;[2] it is normally addressed by an 'I' to a 'Thou', these being for the purposes of reading timeless fictions within the poem, rather than real-life individuals who were born and died. Such conventions make the love-poem evidently a problematic mode for women to practise, and not only because of the obvious difficulty of speaking in a form which defines one as muse, not maker (or as Gilbert and Gubar say of Petrarch's Laura, she 'can never herself be a poet because she "is" *poetry*').[3] Problems also arise from the complex processes of self-definition at work in the classic love-poems. In the great tradition of Petrarch and Shakespeare, the lover-poet is principally concerned with defining his own self through his desire either for the image of his beloved or for his own image mediated through her response to him. What is at stake is not the success or failure of a courtship, but the establishing of an identity through the dialectic of desire and response. Because the complex processes at work within the poems between the poet's 'I' and his muse's 'Thou' (which at once assume gender division and seem to bypass it) cannot be understood in straightforward, common-sense terms, I have devoted a good deal of space to expounding the psychoanalytic constructs without which I do not think this poetry can be fully understood. The question asked in this chapter is not only 'How have women intervened in the tradition of love-sonnets?' but also 'What sort of subjectivities speak and are assumed in these sonnets?' (I am confining the discussion to the sonnet-form, because the sonnet is a traditional but still living medium and a neatly self-defining area.) First, however, it is necessary to outline the psychic processes which these poems articulate.

The relation between poet and mistress-muse in the love-poem repeats, in its characteristic structure and energies, the dyadic relation between mother and infant which the psychoanalyst Jacques Lacan named 'Imaginary'. This term means 'a basically narcissistic relation of the subject to his (sic) ego, a relationship to other subjects as my "counterparts", a relation to the world by means of ideological reflexes; a relation to meaning in terms of resemblance and unity'.[4] The concept of the Imaginary is part of Lacan's complex and influential theory of the structuring of human subjectivity through the acquisition of an identity in language. Although a clear exposition of this topic is next door to impossible, given its inherent complexity and Lacan's notoriously difficult style, a brief summary of the theories of Lacan and his commentators is, however inadequate, useful here.

Imaginary identity is definable, first of all, by reference to Lacan's well-known theory of the 'mirror-phase' (*stade du miroir*), a crucial moment of acquired identity which occurs when a baby (at the age of six months or so) assumes his specular image in the mirror'[5] – a 'recognition' of self that is accompanied by immense pleasure. 'Unable as yet to walk, or even to stand up, and held tightly as he [sic] is by some support, human or artificial ... he nevertheless overcomes, in a flutter of jubilant activity, the obstructions of his support and, fixing his attitude in a slightly leaning-forward position, in order to hold it in his gaze, brings back an instantaneous aspect of the image'.[6] While the baby's body is as yet a helpless, uncoordinated chaos of impulses, its whole, because visible image, is 'the symbolic matrix in which the *I* is precipitated in its primordial form, before it is objectified in the dialectic of identification with the other, and before language restores to it, in the universal, its function as subject'.[7] This primordial 'recognition' of the self is then, a necessary illusion: necessary if the child is to acquire an identity at all, but illusory in that the perfection and completeness of the image deny the infantile helplessness of its actual body. The baby's relation to its mirror-image is 'asymptotic';[8] for this 'primordial matrix' exists at the vanishing-point where representation and reality are imagined as coinciding, but never do.

The term 'Imaginary' does not only refer to the infant's enchantment by its own image; it also describes the earliest relation between mother and child which is the main focus of the Kleinian 'object-relations' school of psychoanalysis. Lacanian discussions of Melanie Klein's theories of infantile identification through the baby's pre-Oedipal relation with her/his mother have been conspicuous by their absence, largely because of Lacan's uncompromising insistence that language defines humanity and that therefore the story of human subjectivity cannot really begin until (to use Lacanian terminology) the child takes up a position in language, its identity as 'he' or 'she' being organized by its relation to the primary signifier of difference: the phallus. In this schema, the Imaginary dyad of mother and baby is no idyll but an emotional deadlock, resolvable only via the 'third term' of language acquisition and castration complex. Sexual difference, signified by the presence or absence of the phallus, is the paradigm of all difference; the Symbolic order of language is itself a system of differences without fixed terms, so that taking up a position in language depends on taking in the concept of difference whose 'privileged signifier' is the phallus: not the actual penis, but the idea or representation of it. The castration complex is thus intimately associated with language acquisition: refusal of the concept of difference means no cosy unitary idyll, but psychosis. (This schema is not to be taken literally: if it were true that everyone must in reality submit to the specifically paternal prohibition of the mother as a no-go area in order to become a speaking 'I', then all children of widows would be speechless psychotics, and David Copperfield owed his sanity to Mr Murdstone's paternal severity.)

The transition from Imaginary to Symbolic can be usefully symbolized by an analogy from grammar. In an Imaginary world, there would only be two possible subjects: 'I' and 'Thou', the first and second person singular. Each of these exists only by virtue of the other: in this mental realm, the 'I' cannot exist without 'Thou' to hear and reflect it, for by itself the 'I' cannot even know what its boundaries are. But 'Thou' is, to the 'I', primarily a means of self-definition reflecting 'I' back to itself. Since to address a '*tu*' always implies the presence of the one invoked, whether s/he is actually there or not,[9] the second person always represents reassurance. There can be communication between this first and second person, but no true speech because they have nothing to speak *about*; their mutual mirroring is a form of deadlock. It is only when the third person 'he, she, it' is introduced that absent things and people can be named – in other words, narrative history can begin. But unlike 'I' and 'Thou', the third person must be identified as 'he' or 'she'; which means that the mastery of absence through language is conditional on the recognition of sexual difference. (Again, I must stress that this grammatical model is intended only as analogy and *not* as explanation of how children actually do learn language: the acquisition of pronouns comes late in this process. In any case, the model only works for Indo-European languages; in a grammar where first and second person were gendered, the analogy would break down.)

But although the entry into language resolves the Imaginary deadlock, language itself, consisting of differences without fixed terms, is a system of displacement and substitution, not of surety. The speaker can master reality and make her/his wishes known, but at the price of internal division: to say 'I' it must split into the self that speaks and the word that is spoken. These processes are illuminated by the psychoanalyst Maud Mannoni's discussion of the famous scene recorded and discussed in Freud's *Beyond the Pleasure Principle*: the fort/da game played by his grandson with a reel and a piece of string, and its variant in which the child played with his reflection in the mirror, *'making himself disappear'*.[10] It is tempting for the newcomer to Lacan to link up this game with the 'mirror-phase' and take it as an example of the way Imaginary processes work. Maud Mannoni argues the opposite:

> The child, as we saw, punctuated with a word what would be interpreted as the rejection and return of the mother. The words 'gone' and 'here' introduced a third dimension – beyond the absence of the real mother, the child began to try out the game of his own disappearance and return, that is, to lay down in relation to his mother's body and his own the bases of his identity. But the field in which he moved was a field of language . . . The object utilized by the child was a matter of no importance; he threw away all small objects in his reach, or substituted a reel. These substitute objects are not symbols but signifiers – they can be anything at all in themselves (they are not representational) . . . The child had absolutely no need, therefore, of a nursery full of toys. *He could contrive to convey his meaning with anything at all.*[11]

This Lacanian account of infantile subjectivity obviously invites the question 'What is the relation between the Imaginary mirror-phase and the Imaginary mother–child dyad?' In the essay 'Stade du miroir' the mother is reduced to a 'human or artificial support': this is presumably a deliberate mockery of the emphasis on the importance of the mother which is characteristic of the imposing 'object-relations' school of psychoanalysis (a kind of argument by contemptuous omission which is fairly frequent in Lacan's writing). But the mother is obviously implied as a participant in the child's self-discovery. Jacqueline Rose has interestingly discussed this point in *Feminine Sexuality*:

> The mirror-image is salutary for the child, since it gives it the first sense of a coherent identity in which it can recognize itself. For Lacan, however, this is already a fantasy – the very image which places the child divides its identity in two. Furthermore, that moment only has meaning in relation to the presence and look of the mother who guarantees its reality for the child. The mother does not as in D.W. Winnicott's account . . . mirror the child to itself; she grants an image *to* the child, which her presence immediately deflects. Holding the child is, therefore, to be understood not only as containing, but as a process of referring, which fractures the unity it seems to offer.[12]

The difficulty of this commentary arises partly from its object of discussion: namely, a psychic process which is approached by deciphering an invisible icon – that is, the tableau of the mother holding her baby up to a mirror. This icon does not exist in D.W. Winnicott's more straightforward model of the mother's *look* as the mirror in which the baby discovers its identity, in which 'the actual mirror has significance mainly in its figurative sense'.[13] In the Lacanian account, the mother at once 'grants the baby an image' and 'deflects it', because although her look (and perhaps smile) are seen in the mirror by the baby at the same time as its own image, her presence is 'split' in the same way as the child, who must connect the feeling of her embrace with its visual counterpart (her mirror-image), and must likewise nego-tiate the gap between the body's feeling of being contained and the mind's identification with the visual image. The image is thus multiplied – or, more accurately, quadrupled, as two pairs (one seen and one felt) of babies and of mothers. The quality of the mother's look becomes relatively unimportant in this account, unlike Winnicott's, for Lacanians and Kleinians respectively date the origin of human identity from different 'moments'. For the latter, the beginning of humanity derives from the infant's early relationship with its mother: 'This beginning perception of the mother as separate, in conjunction with the infant's inner experience of continuity in the midst of changing instances and events, forms the basis for its experience of a self.'[14] For Lacan, human history begins with human speech: the pre-linguistic Imaginary and the Symbolic modes of being are different planes, meeting only at certain 'points de capiton' (gathering points like sofa-buttons). The contrasting key words 'experience' as against 'language' are typical of either side.

The primacy accorded to language in this psychic model explains why Lacanian feminists invariably insist on the conceptual indispensability of the castration complex. If one considers human language to be a system of signifiers constituted purely by difference, and the primordial signifier of difference to be the present/absent phallus, then the acquisition of language must depend on taking in the idea of sexual difference as marked by the presence or absence of that phallus, plus the anxiety and fantasy entailed in these ideas (that is, the castration complex). It will follow that no previous or subsequent experience of presence-in-absence will be meaningful in quite this way: 'Other experiences and perceptions only take their meaning from the law for which it [the castration complex] stands.'[15]

This model of the psyche (inevitably oversimplified in my sketch) is evidently vulnerable to the criticism that it is universalist and ahistorical[16] and that its ready acceptance of such potentially antifeminist notions as the castration complex colludes with the patriarchal bias of their originators instead of deconstructing them – all damaging accusations. Certainly, when Juliet Mitchell insists that both Freud and Lacan are only describing, not endorsing the psychic structures produced by a patriarchal culture, and that the paternal law is to be understood only as metaphor,[17] her arguments are – given the authoritarianism of both men – not very convincing. Nevertheless, these concepts of the Imaginary and Symbolic realms are immensely illuminating as models of human thought and experience; though without direct experience of psychoanalysis (which I have not had) I do not think it possible to accept them as more than models. What is necessary now is to show how this model of an infantile mode of being has to do with questions of identity and relationship between (a) adult lovers and (b) love-sonnets. This is particularly important for understanding the paradoxes and problems of women's approach to the 'I–Thou' lyric, in which presence seems so much more important than gender that it ought to be easy to appropriate, and which is yet so masculine in conception – as the examples discussed in the next section confirm.

2 Mirrors and opposites

> What do I want of Zed? Not his body, merely the whole of him, all the time. It's equivalent to a confession of murder.
>
> (From the diary of T.H. White)[18]

The concept of the Imaginary defines the dynamic of passionate love: idealization, ambivalence, fear and, above all, desire for the beloved total *presence*. The quotation from T.H. White indicates the extremity of one pole of that desire. I would not argue that White's self-scrutiny corresponds to everyone's experience – obviously not, since he had an exceptionally censorious conscience, his sexual inclinations were sadistic, and the fact that his love was not returned may have increased its ambivalence.[19] But that shocking sentence 'It's equivalent to a confession of murder' does not avow a wish to kill: it simply interprets with agonized honesty the lover's desire for total possession of the other's presence – 'the whole of him, all the time', which is a kind of annihilation of his being for all purposes except one's own, and is in that sense 'murder'.

It is also apparent from White's remark that to call the phantasy element in passionate love Imaginary is a comparatively loose description. The difference between the adult, replaying in the relationship of sexual love the infantile dependence, the identification of self in another, and the idealization and anxiety which belong to our earliest experiences, and the baby she or he once was, is not only that the dependence is not so real but that he or she can speak and therefore objectify the experience – as White does. The same point emerges from Barthes's *A Lover's Discourse* in the passage 'Absence' which analyses the way the lover experiences the separation-anxiety of a deserted child:

> In the other's absence, the Other is absent as referent, present as allocutory. From this singular distortion, a kind of insupportable present emerges: you are gone (which I grieve for), you are there (since I address you). I know then what is the present, that difficult tense: a pure portion of anxiety.[20]

While this insight may be accurate, the fact that Barthes can formulate the situation means that, unlike the child experiencing separation, he is not helpless within it. As Lacan writes: 'Language enables [the subject] to see himself as the stage manager or even the producer of any Imaginary trap in which otherwise he would be only a living puppet.'[21] There is all the difference in the world – or at least in the Symbolic order – between the romantic anguish of Barthes's 'Absence', or even of White's diary, and the literally unspeakable emptiness inhabited by

Melanie Klein's analysand 'Dick' or Maud Mannoni's 'Leon', psychotic children without access to meaning.[22] A meditation on absence means that the beloved, even if absent, has a Symbolic existence in words: 'you are there (since I address you)'. Barthes's reflections constitute an infinitely sophisticated version of the 'gone–here' game representing presence in absence: that is, it articulates an Imaginary relationship in Symbolic terms, just as the love-poem does.

But to write of clinical material, Barthes's essays and love-sonnets as if they were interchangeable is obviously questionable. It is true that if you define clinical material as a 'text' to be interpreted, as the Lacanian Maud Mannoni does,[23] then it may be analogous to a poem, but the reverse is by no means true. When dreams or personal histories are interpreted by the psychoanalyst, the analysand is there to extend, contradict or alter the interpretation; similarly, Maud Mannoni's interpretation of Imaginary and Symbolic elements in the 'gone–here' mirror-game is validated by her use of these in interpreting the words of psychotic children. But though a love-lyric may seem like the voice of personal experience, there is no validation from an authorial presence: the poet seems directly 'there' in the poem and yet is not available, for the 'I' of a lyric poem, as all students of poetry learn, is a fiction. To assume that this 'I' equals a historical person to whose unconscious motives one has a privileged access by virtue of knowing, say, Freud and Lacan, would be a quick road to authoritarian misreading. In fact, very little psychoanalytic attention has been focused on to love-poems.[24] The most influential works of deconstruction have been directed at nineteenth-century realist fiction, Romantic autobiographical poems or modernist texts,[25] while love-poems are recalcitrant material for any reading that takes a hermeneutic approach, in that, lacking any narrative, they contain no apparent history whose hidden meaning can be deciphered. The I-Thou dyad on which the love-sonnet is structured puts it outside any story; the only way it can be turned into a case-history, and its secrets detected, is to construct a personality and history for the poet out of her/his poems. When we are reading the work of a poet we can, of course, hardly help doing this as a method of assimilation and understanding, but as a method of exegesis it is likely to tell us more about the mind of the critic than the poems criticized.[26]

And the business of interpreting love-sonnets by psychoanalytic constructs is, however important, not made easier by the fact that these are themselves often slippery. For example, two distinguished authorities, defining the nature of the love-relationship, apparently contradict each other as to the phantasied gender of the lover versus the beloved. Freud suggests that the lover is always masculine: in 'A Case of Female Homosexuality' he writes of his patient that 'in her behaviour to her love-object she had throughout assumed the masculine part: that is to say, she displayed the humility and the sublime overvaluation of the sexual object so characteristic of the male lover, the renunciation of all narcissistic satisfaction, and the preference for being the lover rather than the beloved.'[27] Roland Barthes, on the other hand, assigns to the lover the role of the woman who waits: 'in every man who speaks the absence of the other, the *feminine* (principle) declares itself: this man who waits and who suffers from it, is miraculously feminized.'[28] Since both the love affairs in these analyses are homosexual, it would be neat to solve the problem by suggesting that the inverted lover simply changes his or her mental sex – neat, but untrue, since what is being defined is a position in Imaginary phantasy which can be adopted by a heterosexual or homosexual person of either gender.

It is, one might argue, paradoxical that the question of the lover's gender in poetry should arise at all, since the Imaginary I–Thou dyad seems to exist outside these categories: the difficulty could be seen as an illusion consequent on the mistake of applying analyses of actual lovers to the presences applied in a poem. This argument could only work, however, if the I–Thou dyad functioned outside of the Symbolic order of language – which is even less possible for a poem than for people. And since the great tradition of love-poems is masculine in origin, it is not surprising that, as far as poetry is concerned, Freud is right: the love-sonnet does manifest its mediaeval origin in characteristically presenting a heterosexual relationship in which the beloved, assigned the role of passive reflecting Other, is thereby feminized (a point argued in more detail in the discussion of one of Shakespeare's sonnets, below). For in any poem where the lover's self is being defined in and through a relationship with a beloved, that process of definition implies the masculinity of the lover and the femininity of the other; which is why, as we shall see, the love-poem presents problems to women poets.

But the problem of defining psychic identities *in a poem* is still unresolved in this argument. To attempt such a resolution, I am drawing on Frederick Goldin's study of the role of the mirror-image in mediaeval courtly lyrics, *The Mirror of Narcissus*, a book which is most illuminating in its treatment of the relation between desire, image and identity. Goldin's most significant point for my purposes is his analysis of the poet's identification of the beloved lady with a reflecting mirror. In what Goldin calls the 'mirror-lyrics', the mirror is not always identified by name; nevertheless often 'the presence of an image, in these texts, presupposes the existence of a mirror'[29] – an image which articulates a deep ambivalence, (corresponding to its dual status in the Platonic thought which Goldin finds at work within the poems), between brute, formless matter and the ideal image which it contains 'As the mirror is made of matter, it has the capacity of matter to receive the image of ideal forms'[30] – but the mirror can only reflect the ideal, not become it.

Although the lady in the courtly poems is 'a localization of the ideal, an image that accommodates the infirmities of secular life',[31] she is imperfect because she is human. The lady as mirror is, then, the instrument of idealization: 'what we see in the mirror is not so much an exact likeness of the object as its perfected form, its ideal.'[32] She thus at once incarnates the ideal of courtly society and shows the lover his ideal self, the man who, through her service, he is to become; she is 'the standard by which all things are judged, the ideal light by which they are known'.[33] But, 'before it is possible to call her a mirror, a great psychic event has taken place: the courtly ideal and all the doctrines that define it have been translated into a visible form in the immediate image of the lady . . . The self-image is as elusive as the reflected image in the fountain, but the lady lives and can be possessed. Thus the idealization of the lady saves the lover from the thirst and despair of Narcissus, from loving what cannot live.'[34] But if the mirror cracks, then so does the lover's self: 'Unreflected, he is socially and morally invisible.'[35]

The identity articulated in these courtly poems is evidently related to but not the same as Lacan's Imaginary mirror-image, and not only because, unlike the latter, it reflects a social ideal. The relation between desire and identity here is almost the reverse of Lacan's: in the Old French poem *Narcisus*, which Goldin expounds as a model of the courtly lover's self-awareness, it is the hero's experience of pain arising from the knowledge that the desiring self is separate from the desired image, that awakens self-awareness in him. Narcisus is hardly aware of himself as a person until his love for the image arouses him: to recognize its beauty as his own, he has to become aware of his own body's demands. This is almost a mirror-reversal of what happens in the *stade du miroir*, where the infant, whose experience of its own body is chaotic, assumes a unified but alienated identity in its mirror-image. There is all the difference here between waking up, as Narcisus does, to the consciousness of the body one has been all along, and identifying oneself with an imaginary double (and repressing the process). All of this implies that the 'mirror-lyric' needs to be understood within its social and historical context, as specific to a particular mediaeval class: one cannot assume that the figure of the mirror means exactly the same thing in, say, a Renaissance sonnet sequence, let alone a poem written in 1930, as it does in the lyrics translated and discussed by Goldin. On the other hand, Goldin argues that the 'mirror-lyrics' retain their interest because they raise what he calls the 'timeless questions: "How does a man know whether he is what he thinks he is? And how does he know whether he is becoming what he wants to be?" '[36] It is remarkable how unconsciously androcentric these questions are ('man' = 'human' even when, as here, both experience and ego-ideal are specifically masculine). In the mirror lyrics, the lady's experience and identity do not matter at all; she is the gaze that makes the knight real to himself, and what *she* sees and what *she* wants are out of the picture altogether: the question 'How does a woman know whether she is what she thinks she is?' does not arise. (If a woman is shown looking into a mirror, this is simply the sign of her feminine vanity.) In their blind spot for female experience, both the poems and, still more, the Platonic material which Goldin cites as the key to their interpretation, offer startlingly apt confirmation of the arguments proposed by the feminist psychoanalyst Luce Irigaray in *Speculum*, especially the essay 'Une Mère de glace', that Platonic philosophical discourse excludes women from its conceptual world by associating man with human reason, woman with matter as the passive formless mirror which exists to reflect the unified, idealized image of masculine intelligence. The lady of the mirror-lyrics, who is the 'passive and glorified instrument of the lover's desire, reflecting what she does not truly possess'[37] corresponds to Irigaray's contention that woman exists in masculine discourse only as an Other passively reflecting a masculine ego-ideal.[38] If Irigaray is right, then the consequence for the love-poem of Western man's obsession with his own morally and intellectually visible identity will be the association of otherness with femininity. In a poem where the speaker establishes an identity through his relationship with another person, that person, reduced to a necessary presence, is denied full humanity and is thus feminized in the sense of being rendered negative – made into a blank Platonic mirror. To put the matter in Freudian terms, the Imaginary demand that the loved one be the consciousness that validates the lover's own self is a form of castration: what T.H. White melodramatically styled 'murder'. This diagnosis can be clarified by looking closely at a traditional classic: Shakespeare's Sonnet 71:

No longer mourn for me when I am dead
Than you shall hear the surly sullen bell
Give warning to the world that I am fled
From this vile world, with vilest worms to dwell.
Nay, if you read this line, remember not
The hand that writ it, for I love you so
That I in your sweet thoughts would be forgot
If thinking on me then should make you woe.
O if, I say, you look upon this verse
When I perhaps commingled am with clay,
Do not so much as my poor name rehearse
But let your love even with my life decay.
Lest the wise world should look into your moan
And mock you with me after I am gone.

Such expressions of totally unselfish love have caused the *Sonnets* to be considered as sublime monuments of passionate goodwill, 'a region where love abandons all claims and flowers into charity'.[39] But the love expressed here appears more devious and contradictory the more closely one examines it. This is partly because of the way the poem counterposes matter and spirit, the corruptible materiality of the poet's body set against his lover's 'sweet thoughts'. The beloved is not here (as often in the *Sonnets*) a personification of physical and moral beauty, but a presence – a consciousness which the poem needs to make itself intelligible; he is represented not as a physical being but as possessing the capacity for hearing, memory, sight and speech (not, one notes, for loving). These faculties, of course, imply his existence as a living body (he will need eyes to read the poem), but the emphasis is on him as the perceiving mind which will register the physical traces of the poet's remains – the poet looking forward to a time when there will be nothing left of him except a decaying corpse – and, of course, his own words. 'Nay, if you read this line, remember not / The hand that writ it' calls up both the dead hand of the corpse the poet will become, and the live hand writing in the 'dramatic present' of the poem.

Its contradictory nature is plain on the simplest level: proposing to its recipient an oblivion which it renders impossible, it reminds him to ignore its own words. This unselfishness, oddly, crowds out the beloved from the poem's own moral space; the cold-hearted egotism proposed for him in the last couplet is in sharp contrast to the poet's own gesture of renunciation: 'lest the wise world should look into your moan / And mock you with me after I am gone.' The world has become 'wise' instead of 'vile'; if the poet is mocked it must be because of his unworldly generosity. The beloved, in loving what no longer exists, would be just such a generous fool; he is therefore warned against the pain of love. But if the experience of loving is good for the poet, why not for his beloved? There is something dubious about a generosity which excludes the possibility of an equal response from its object; and there is a curious dissonance between the idealization of the beloved's 'sweet thoughts' and the shallow response proposed for him, which has nothing to do with the question of whether the real-life original actually was a cold-hearted egotist. He scarcely exists in the poem except – crucially – as a consciousness: as the place where the poet defines his own generous identity. The poem needs that consciousness for its words to take on coherence and meaning: in the beloved's look they will come to life. This is not, of course, a 'real' look:

> O if, I say, you look upon this verse
> When I perhaps commingled am with clay,
> Do not so much as my poor name rehearse . . .

What is needed here is what is denied: the possibility of the beloved reading, remembering and speaking – that is, not his actual presence, but the idea of it. This sonnet is, then, not only a classic of English poetry but also a classic 'mirror-poem', not in the sense of playing through imagery of reflection (as others of Shakespeare's *Sonnets* do),[40] but as a poem enacting an Imaginary relationship in which the being of the person addressed must always be at least partially denied or ignored, both because it is finally unknowable and because it is overlaid with the excitement of Imaginary phantasies in which 'Thou' exists to reflect 'I' back to itself.

I have extracted this poem from its Elizabethan context, discussing it as though the relation between its 'I' and 'Thou' existed out of history, because its importance for my argument is as a poetic model. Shakespeare himself constitutes a major part of the literary context for the poets I am considering in the rest of this chapter: Edna St Vincent Millay and Christina Rossetti. For these women, Shakespeare's sonnets are simply 'there': timeless masterpieces which any cultivated person had read, and of which their own poems are in a sense rewritings; it is therefore useful to examine how one of these 'timeless masterpieces' created and defined the ways sexual love can be imagined in poetry. I do not mean by this to claim that I read the sonnet in the same way that Edna St

Vincent Millay did; on the contrary, my purpose is to explore how women poets negotiated the Imaginary motifs of masculine poetic tradition to write their own versions of love-poems, when they probably did not name that tradition to themselves as 'masculine' at all.

3 Romantic transcendence: Edna St Vincent Millay

There is a good-tempered but patronizing poem by Kingsley Amis which suggests that, contrary to my own arguments above, the love-poem is a characteristically female mode:

> *Landscape near Parma*
> Interests a man, so does *The Double Vortex*,
> So does *Rilke and Buddha*.

> 'I travel, you see', 'I think', and 'I can read',
> These titles seem to say,
> But *I Remember You, Love Is My Creed,*
> *Poem for J.,*

> The ladies choice . . .[41]

. . . Is trickier and less predictable than it looks, women having arrived comparatively late in the tradition of love-poetry. Nevertheless, Edna St Vincent Millay, best known for her love poems, does appear to correspond to the pattern suggested by Amis, though she is by no means as naive as his parody. She also follows on appropriately from Shakespeare in that her poetic approach is traditional in a straightforward sense. The experiments of Modernism passed her by; despite the freedom and colloquialism of her later work, she uses mainly Romantic conventions. The ready intelligibility of her poems, especially to readers with expectations formed by knowledge of the poetry of Keats, Shelley, Tennyson, Milton and

Shakespeare, accounts both for her once immense popularity and for the shortage of serious criticism of her work, which is celebrated for its resounding declarations of passion and its ease of comprehension. Her poems are thoroughly pleasurable texts.

Millay's best-known sequence of love-sonnets, *Fatal Interview*, depends on an individual voice speaking with a poetic vocabulary (thematic as well as lexical) which is drawn from Elizabethan poetry as reread by the Romantics, as in sonnet VIII:

> Yet in an hour to come, disdainful dust,
> You shall be bowed and brought to bed with me.
> While the blood roars, or when the blood is rust
> About a broken engine, this shall be.
> If not today, then later; if not here,
> On the green grass, with sighing and delight,
> Then under it, all in good time, my dear,
> We shall be laid together in the night.

The poet's confidence and ease in handling the sonnet form are immediately apparent; she slides effortlessly from the twentieth-century image of 'rust / About a broken engine' to the 'timeless' line 'On the green grass, with sighing and delight', using the associative rhymes 'rust' and 'dust' and the emphatic alliteration of 'bowed and brought to bed' with an effect of relish, not cliché. Her appropriation of literary tradition is equally apparent in the way that the counterposing of love and death, the brevity of human life and the sleep of the grave, recalls Shakespeare, Marvell and Catullus[42] in a *cantabile* lyricism formed on Keats. This is not an allusive poem; rather, its themes are smoothed with poetic handling, and it is written in a style which assumes that poetry is timeless (which is *not*, of course, to say that the poem is timeless in itself). Not that Millay's virtue as a poet lies exactly in her skill at recuperating crashed cars into Romantic convention; it is the energy of her declaration of desire that gives the poem a punch which is assisted by her confident ease:

> And ruder and more violent, be assured,
> Than the desirous body's heat and sweat
> That shameful kiss by more than night obscured
> Wherewith at last the scornfullest mouth is met.

On the level of argument, this logic is shaky; but as fantasy it succeeds completely; the poem is a celebration of sexual energy that works through entertaining the idea of death, without being at all necrophilic. What is invoked is not an ironic parody of sex, as in 'Then worms shall try / That long preserv'd virginity', nor a negation as in Catullus' 'nox est perpetua una dormienda' ('we have one perpetual night to sleep through'); it works as promise rather than threat – 'all in good time, my dear, / We shall be laid together in the night.' The sexual energy of 'the desirous body's heat and sweat' is actually outbid by the 'ruder and more violent ... shameful kiss' – a remarkably passionate assault from the cold earth. It is as if the idea of death and its denial of sexuality is for Millay a means of contradictorily allowing the pleasure principle to win out.

This poetry has a splendid resonance, well evoked by Edmund Wilson's reminiscence of first reading a Millay sonnet, 'which I immediately got by heart and found myself declaiming in the shower'[43] – the attraction of Millay's style being apparent in Wilson's evidently unconscious lapse into iambic pentameters. The declamatory vigour is inseparable from the sexuality; Millay's easy familiarity with the themes and techniques of the past does not mean that she uses them as ingredients in a unisex rhetoric of passion. This poem, like many of her others, succeeds as a statement of female desire, and its bold references to lovemaking break consciously with Victorian conventions of purity and high-mindedness. Yet though it is full of embracing and touch, the poem is most passionate when engaged by an impossible fantasy, which perhaps suggests an emotional liberation less complete than the defiant sexiness of the opening lines would imply.

It is noticeable that the man addressed is very little of a presence in the poem; all we know of him is that the poet has not yet seduced him. Edmund Wilson is shrewd here: 'When she came to write about her lovers, she gave then so little individuality that it was usually, in any given case, impossible to tell which man she was writing about. What interests her is seldom the people themselves, but her own emotions about them.'[44] This last is probably true of all writers of love-poems; the difference between Millay and her masculine predecessors is that she does not idealize her lover into a beautiful Other, nor into a presence she needs to establish her own identity. Rather, a recurring pattern is discernible in Millay's first-person love-poems (not only *Fatal Interview*) of herself as ardently loving and her lover as grudgingly unresponsive. The passion expressed is often felt as inappropriate to its object:

> I being born a woman and distressed
> By all the needs and motions of my kind,
> Am urged by your propinquity to find
> Your person fair, and feel a certain zest
> To bear your body's weight upon my breast:
> So subtly is the fume of life designed
> To clarify the pulse and cloud the mind.[45]

The *donnée* of most of her poems, that she loves more and he less, can have bad poetic results, as with the embarrassing 'You loved me not at all, but let it pass; / I loved you more than life, but let it be' (*Fatal Interview* XL) — a classic of self-conscious generosity tipping over into self-pity. Where Millay's sonnets construct an identity for the self that speaks, it is not to be found in the other's response but in the experience of loving, as in

Fatal Interview VII, which records the absence of the loved one:

> Night is my sister, and how deep in love,
> How drowned in love and weedily washed ashore,
> There to be fretted by the drag and shove
> Of the tide's edge, I lie – these things, a more:
> Whose arm along between me and the sand,
> Whose voice alone, whose pitiful breath brought near
> Could thaw these nostrils and unlock this hand
> She could advise you, should you care to hear.

The power of this poem is its vivid re-creation of bodily desire worked out in the felt detail of the metaphors of drowning: the 'drag and shove / Of the tide's edge' and the cramped fingers are extraordinarily apt images for a body at the mercy of the frustrated ache for a lover's touch. This, however, will not be granted:

> Small chance, however, in a storm so black
> A man will leave his friendly fire and snug
> For a drowned woman's sake, and bring her back
> To drip and scatter shells upon the rug.
>
> (VII)

Interestingly, Millay reverses the usual roles of man and woman here: he is a domesticated creature who doesn't want his room messed up, while the image of the drowned woman scattering shells gives her the strangeness of a sea-creature – appropriately enough, since the stormy sea is a metaphor for her turbulent depths. He is not equal to her challenge, and she does not expect an adequate response: the poem is written as if to someone who cannot or will not hear. (It is a pity that the last couplet – always a problem in the Shakespearian sonnet – collapses into redundant adjectives and the pathetic fallacy: 'Only the Night, with tears on her dark face / Watches beside me in this windy place.') The man's absence, his obtuseness and her desire for him structure the poem.

Fatal Interview (1931), from which the sonnets I have discussed are taken, is a sequence of fifty-two sonnets dramatizing particular moments in an unhappy love affair; it is a little like Meredith's *Modern Love*, but done from the woman's point of view. As with all achieved sonnet sequences, the poems gain a great deal from being read in the order in which they are set out. The affair begins with the man indifferent and the woman frustrated (as in sonnets VII and VIII quoted above); sonnet XI, which marks the transition to a precarious happiness, takes the form of an offer:

> Love in the open hand, no thing but that,
> Ungemmed, unhidden, wishing not to hurt
> As one should bring you cowslips in a hat
> Swung from the hand, or apples in a skirt,
> I bring you, calling out as children do
> 'Look what I have! – And these are all for you.'

It is comparatively rare for these sonnets to be so dramatic; more often, they are soliloquies. The few dramatized scenes between the lovers are mostly those celebrating lovemaking:

> O sweet, O heavy-lidded, O my love . . .
> Be not discountenanced if the knowing know
> We rose from rapture half an hour ago.

> (XXVIII)

Happiness is never untroubled and soon goes; the woman's half-conscious fears of rejection ('Sorrowful dreams, remembered after waking', XXXIII) are quickly justified: the man comes to resent her ('I surmise / My kisses now are sand against your mouth, / Teeth in your palm and pennies on your eyes', XXXIX). She is left unrepentant, but with wounds that will never quite heal.

A recent article by Jane Stanborough on Millay's

poetry reads *Fatal Interview* as a prolonged cautionary tale of feminine naivety – 'an extended metaphorical illustration of the consequences to women of their susceptibility to emotional exploitation'.[46] For this critic, the woman's fatal flaw is her need for romantic love. She quotes sonnet XVII in evidence of this theme, stressing the irony of the woman's 'willing surrender to rape and murder':[47]

Sweet love, sweet thorn, when lightly to my heart
I took your thrust, whereby I since am slain
And lie dishevelled on the grass apart,
A sodden thing bedrenched by tears and rain,
While rainy evening drips to misty night
And misty night to cloudy morning clears,
And clouds disperse across the gathering light
And birds grow noisy, and the sun appears –
Had I bethought me then, sweet love, sweet thorn,
How sharp an anguish even at the best
When all's requited and the future sworn
The happy hour can leave within the breast
 I had not then come running at the call
 Of one who loves me little, if at all.

          (XVII)

I agree with Jane Stanborough that the point of this poem is the woman's discovery of her own insignificance, but this is a more complex and less pathetic process than her emphasis on Millay's vulnerability suggests. The poems preceding this one (XII, XV, XVI) allude to Greek legends of love between gods and humans (*Fatal Interview* is full of such classical reference, beginning and ending with a goddess enthralled by a man). In this context, the image of one lying on the ground 'slain by a thrust' recalls Adonis, the beautiful boy who refused Venus's love and was killed by the thrust of the boar he chose to hunt instead. In this version, it is the woman who suffers the wound; the man has the indifference and (by implication) the proverbial beauty of Adonis, and the woman has his pathos and Venus's desire. Female sensuality and male indifference remain central to the story, but with a twist: unlike Venus, the woman does seduce her 'sweet love', but the experience is destructive because what means much to her means little to him. What happens is not rape – 'lightly to my heart / I *took* your thrust' (my italics) but penetration by a careless man who is clearly willing to fuck an eager woman. The terms on which she can have him deny her more completely than simple frustration would have done, hence the metaphorical 'mortal wound'. The speaker is plainly not dying – she is lying awake all night in confused misery, imaged as usual in Millay by darkness, mist and rain, which is not dissipated but clarified by daybreak. The culmination of the poem is not her immediate misery but her understanding of it. The sonnet thus enacts a partial victory over experience: the poet knows why she suffers and has used ancient legend to articulate her knowledge, thereby giving the experience itself something of a classical status. (Something similar is done on Sonnet XII, a monologue imagining her lover as Zeus, no less.)

Unquestionably, the experience itself is painful, and the fact that the 'murder' turns out to be the little death of orgasm plus postcoital gloom, and the 'rape' to be penetration by an uncaring man, would seem to support Jane Stanborough's argument that the whole sequence is really a warning against 'the spiritual disintegration that must occur through the social conditioning that explains woman's nature as essentially emotional and her greatest need as love'.[48] The difficulty is that this analysis is too ironic and disillusioned to fit Millay's poetry; the sonnets are committed to a Romanticism that includes an ideal of passionate love, *not* to questioning that ideal. In poem after poem Millay asserts the value of the experience of loving, whatever pain it may bring:

> Heart, have no pity in this house of bone,
> Shake it with dancing, break it down with joy.
> (XXIX)

This commitment inspires some of her grandest rhetorical gestures:

> It may well be that in a difficult hour
> Pinned down by pain and moaning for release,
> Or nagged by want past resolution's power,
> I might be driven to sell your love for peace,
> Or trade the memory of this night for food.
> It well may be. I do not think I would.
>
> (XXX)

The rejection which comes all too soon produces not disintegration in the woman but a kind of confidence: the declarations of passion grow in certainty and even arrogance:

> I know my mind and I have made my choice . . .
> Your presence and your favours, the full part
> That you could give, you now can take away:
> What lies between your beauty and my heart
> Not even you can trouble or betray.
>
> (XLV)

Or, in more muted but still confident tones:

> If I had loved you less or played you slyly
> I might have held you for a summer more,
> But at the cost of words I value highly
> And no such summer as the one before.
> Should I outlive this anguish – and men do –
> I shall have only good to say of you.
>
> (XLVII)

Such bold declarations are not the whole story: the assertion 'I shall have only good to say of you' is followed by two sonnets of desolation. Even here, though, the poet keeps her balance:

> But pain to such degree and of such kind
> As I must suffer if I think of you,
> Not in my senses will I undergo.
>
> (XLIX)

This combines vulnerability with tough precision; the speaker faces her pain in the very act of 'refusing' to name it, and the dangerous word 'you' is actually emphasized by the rhyme-scheme. On the other hand, the relationship between heroine and lover in *Fatal Interview*, as in the later *Theme with Variations*, is unequal. The man has all the coldness and power to frustrate of the original distant ladies in courtly love-poems, and none of their virtue; while the heroine's defiant transgression of conventional sexual mores makes her even more vulnerable emotionally than her passionate generous sensitivity would make her anyway. As a scenario for a relationship this recalls the more bitter monologues of Dorothy Parker like 'The Telephone', or the novels of Jean Rhys in which emancipated women are exploited by sexy cynical men. But Millay's poems do not question their own terms (that is, a commitment to Romantic love matched by an appropriately traditional technique); their adherence to – *not* parody of – tradition is an implicit claim for unhindered speech, a denial that there is any dissonance between being a woman and being a poet, a claim endorsed by Edmund Wilson in appropriately Romantic terms: 'In giving expression to profoundly felt personal experience, she was able to identify herself with more general human experience and stand forth as spokesman for the human spirit.'[49] Wilson's assumption that the poet is a transcendent subject representing the 'human spirit' (recognizably connected to Wordsworth's formulation of the poet as representing humanity: 'man speaking to men') accurately describes the direction and energies of Millay's work. And the Romantic belief articulated by Wilson and presumably shared by Millay, that poetry is the articulation of a straightforward subjectivity ('the expression of profoundly felt personal experience') explains why the poems state rather than explore the identity of the heroine. Her lover is the occasion of the poems, not the presence which confirms and in a sense creates her self; he is too unsatisfactory to function as an

Imaginary ideal mirror. These sonnets offer a series of admirably dramatized moments, not a definition of identity through the presence of the other.

4 Self-definition by renunciation: Christina Rossetti

Christina Rossetti's short sonnet sequence 'Monna Innominata' ('Unnamed lady') enacts a literal rewriting of poetic tradition. In the note prefacing the sequence, the poet explains that it is an imaginary reply to Dante or Petrarch (qutations from whom preface each poem) by a representative Muse – that is, the woman behind the poems. Dante's Beatrice and Petrarch's Laura 'have come down to us resplendent with charms but (at least to my apprehension) scant of individual attractiveness ... One can imagine many a lady sharing her lover's poetic aptitude ... [and] had such a lady spoken for herself, the portrait left us might have appeared more tender if less dignified.'[50] Ellen Moers describes this poetry as sounding 'as if that lady in Shakespeare who never told her love got down off her rock, where she had been sitting like patience all these centuries, and began to speak like this:

> 'Love me, for I love you' – and answer me
> 'Love me, for I love you': so shall we stand
> As happy equals in the flowering land
> Of love, that knows not a dividing sea.'[51]

Not that this note of triumph (from Sonnet VII) is all that frequent in the sequence, whose discernible narrative element is a bleak one, as its preface promises ('assuming the barrier between them to be held sacred by both'):[52] the story begins with the man's absence and ends with his final disappearance, leaving the heroine middle-aged, unloved and resigned to disappointment. It is hinted that her love outlasts his, and all through the sonnets, love is permitted but satisfaction is not.

As one would expect in poems consciously recasting

traditional material, there are points of difference between these sonnets and their originals. Unlike Dante, Petrarch and the poets of the mirror-lyric, Christina Rossetti's sonnets do not present an idealized image of the lover; on the contrary, she hints a criticism of the way such poetry distorts what it idealizes: 'I loved and guessed at you, you construed me / And loved me for what might or might not be', IV). To construe is to interpret, but also to construct: Rossetti refuses to imposes her own constructions on the other. In consequence, the emphasis is all on the heroine's subjectivity, since we are told very little about the attributes of the lover; he is not made a model of physical or moral beauty. This is partly, of course, a product of Victorian high-mindedness: because the speaker never voices desire for her lover's body, only for his presence, he is bound to be somewhat shadowy. Even sonnet III, which reworks the traditional theme of the lover appearing in dreams to a sleeper who wakes to 'find with dreams the dear companion gone', makes the dream include an exchange not of embraces but looks: 'I hold you full in sight, / I blush again who waking look so wan.' And since the sequence is premised on the assumption (derived from its originals) that the lady's role is a passive one of waiting and watching, the man cannot be assigned Laura's or Beatrice's role of simply *being* virtue or beauty, or the poems would have no dynamic at all. The lover's personality is undetectable; his love is never doubted, but all the poems except sonnet VI, which answers his reproof of the lady for possibly idolizing him, seem to be spoken when he is not present. He emerges on the whole as a kind of loving absence.

Consistently with her refusal to put the man up on a pedestal as he has done her, the 'Unnamed Lady' insists (as in the quotation cited by Ellen Moers) on the equality of love. This is put most strongly in sonnet XI:

> But by my heart of love laid bare to you,
> My love that you can make not void or vain,

> Love that forgoes you but to claim anew
> Beyond this passage of the gate of death,
> I charge you at the Judgment, make it plain
> My love for you was life and not a breath.

It is appropriate that this declaration of equality should put into question, however obliquely, the masculine poet's traditional monopoly of representation. 'I charge you at the Judgment, *make it plain*', she commands, acknowledging that he is the one who will tell the story of their love. And as the occasion for the 'Monna Innominata' itself indicates, he did not tell the full truth.

Consequently, these sonnets do not play through the drama of courtship and passion, nor does the lady soliloquize about whether her love is returned. She speaks from a secure position, but one of deprivation. And in so far as the poems construct her identity, they do so not, as in their originals, by examining the speaker's own responses to the ideal image of the lover in her mind (as we have seen, Christina Rossetti avoids 'construing' such an image), but through the experience of passively loving. The lover is not a mirror to the woman poet who addresses him; rather, these sonnets represent the process of offering oneself as a mirror to the other.

Deprivation and absence are constant themes in these poems. It is not just that they often mention frustration – 'Thinking of you, and all that was, and all / That might have been and now can never be' (IX) or 'Love and parting in exceeding pain' (XI). Their fascination lies in the way they explore the intertwining of desire and absence. This is the explicit theme of sonnet I:

> Come back to me, who wait and watch for you:
> Or come not yet, for it is over then
> And long it is before you come again,
> So far between my pleasures are and few.
> While, when you come not, what I do I do
> Thinking 'Now when he comes', my sweetest 'when':

> For one man is my world of all the men
> This wide world holds: O love, my world is you.

The language of this sonnet imitates the speaker's mentally active passivity; in 'What I do I do / Thinking, "Now when he comes" ', the second 'I do', which grammatically speaking controls the sentence, is actually drained of significance by its qualifiers. Though the syntax is careful and Latinate, the repetition 'I do I do' – a purposive verb becoming a babble – has an absurdity emphasized by the enjambment, which nearly disrupts the sense. A different kind of repetition, which valorizes a word instead of parodying it, exists in the variations 'come back . . . come back yet . . . you come again . . . when you come not . . . when he comes'. This loving, obsessive repetition indicates how sweetness gets attached to the words that are talismans of the lover's presence, desire being displaced on to signifiers like the word of promise, 'my sweetest "when" '. These repetitions make for a curious, spartan style, not prolix but narrowly intense:

> For one man is my world of all the men
> This wide world holds: O love, my world is you.

This quintessentially Imaginary fantasy exploits a lexical ambiguity: the man represents for her the whole human world, but as humanity = men, this simply consists of an infinity of versions of the one man she cares for. This way of writing makes one much aware of the intrinsic emptiness of signifiers in the way the speaker's mind clings to the most general words – 'you', 'world', 'man', 'when' – because her desire has made them substitutes for the presence that is their true signified. The tenderness of 'O love, my world is you' is countered by the appalling narrowness of the experience presented: solitude, desire and deprivation. Absence and lack characterize even the most straightforward of the sonnets:

I wish I could remember that first day,
First hour, first moment of your meeting me . . .
If only I could recollect it, such
A day of days! I let it come and go,
As traceless as a thaw of bygone snow;
It seemed to mean so little, meant so much;
If only now I could recall that touch,
First touch of hand in hand! Did one but know!

(II)

Pleasure never appears directly in any of these poems. Just as, in another sonnet, the forbidden words 'I hold you' are concealed in a narrative of visual illusion ('In happy dreams I hold you full in sight', III) so here the idea of even the most token sexual satisfaction – 'First touch of hand!' – is represented through the experience of its loss. The occasion of the poem not only is distant in time but has disappeared from memory because it was never registered; desire makes the 'touch' significant, but only *after* it has become intangible. The line 'As traceless as a thaw of bygone snow' shows this contradictory relation between loss and desire: the simile connotes virgin coldness melting into sexual warmth, but its meaning is loss and disappearance. Again, it is the word 'touch', not the real-life formal handshake to which it refers, that carries the intensity of desire to recapture that unreachable moment.

As this discussion suggests, the 'Monna Innominata' sonnets lend themselves easily to being read in terms of a Lacanian understanding of feminine sexuality. This is partly owing to their religious dimension whereby God is the transcendent presence that structures the relationship between the heroine's 'I' and her lover's 'Thou', not least in the divine probition, 'held sacred by both', against their love's fulfilment. The consequent absence of the lover so dominates the poems that desire becomes attached, as we have seen, to the signifiers themselves; the poems' preoccupation with their own words marks them as belonging to the Symbolic realm defined by the paternal prohibition against full enjoyment of the desired object. This prohibition is connected with the woman speaker's sense of herself as defined by lack, 'helpless to help and impotent to do' (XIII). Even when she appears to propose an orthodox Imaginary identification in sonnet V – 'O my heart's heart, and you who are to me / More than myself', – she goes on to propose opposite destinies; for him, God's service, for her 'to love you much and yet to love you more . . . since woman is the helpmeet made for man'. In other words, her destiny is not action but desire. But even here, she claims no transcendence; his true goal is not her but God, 'Whose love your love's capacity can fill'. Only if she yields the man to God's higher claim is she allowed the partial satisfaction of loving him. Full enjoyment is out of the question.

These complexities of submission to divine paternal law, lack and failure in the self, and female desire can be connected with a passionate early poem of Christina Rossetti's, expressing a desire so excessive that no human response can possibly answer it:

> To give, to give, not to receive!
> I long to pour myself, my soul,
> Not to keep back or count or leave.
> But king with king to give the whole.
> I long for one to stir my deep –
> I have had enough of help and gift –
> I long for one to search and sift
> Myself, to take myself and keep.
>
> You scratch my surface with your pin
> You stroke me smooth with hushing breath:
> Nay pierce, nay probe, nay dig within,
> Probe my quick core and sound my depth.

You call me with a puny call,
You talk, you smile, you nothing do:
How should I spend my heart on you
My heart that so outweighs you all?

. . . .

Not in this world of hope deferred,
This world of perishable stuff:-
Eye hath not seen nor ear hath heard
Nor heart conceived that full 'enough':
Here moans the separating sea,
Here harvests fail, here breaks the heart:
There God shall join and no man part
I full of Christ and Christ of me.
('The Heart Knoweth Its Own Bitterness', 1857)[53]

This poem is almost like a verbal equivalent of the Bernini statue *St Teresa in Ecstasy* illustrating Lacan's seminar '*Encore*' on feminine sexuality.[54] The fantasy of desire for a transcendent plentitude 'that full "enough" ', the quotation from the marriage service, the phallic imagery articulating the exasperation at the human lover's impotence – 'You scratch my surface with your pin ... nay pierce, nay probe, nay dig ...' – are too evident to need much commentary. The difference between this poem and the 'Monna Innominata' sonnets is not only the obvious one of tone and form, nor the sonnets' lack of the conscious vitality and untapped energy that fill the earlier poem, but that the fulfilment imagined in the splendidly passionate 'I full of Christ and Christ of me' has disappeared. There is nothing left but desire prolonged in a solitude which by the last sonnet has become complete.

Though readers of Rossetti who are already familiar with 'Goblin Market' do not need to be told that she is a major poet of female sexuality, I do not claim her sonnets as definitive expressions of feminine desire. It would be perverse to claim this of poetry so much marked by the limiting conventions of its time, which determine, for example, the way the lady of the sonnets is much aware of her own appearance, twice finding fault with it.[55] The most interesting treatment of this theme occurs in sonnet XIV, which ends the sequence:

> Youth gone, and beauty gone, if ever there
> Dwelt beauty in so poor a face as this;
> Youth gone and beauty, what remains of bliss?
> I will not bind fresh roses in my hair
> To shame a cheek at best but little fair . . .
> Youth gone, and beauty gone, what doth remain?
> The longing of a heart pent up forlorn
> A silent heart whose silence loves and longs;
> The silence of a heart which sang its songs
> While youth and beauty made a summer morn,
> Silence of love that cannot sing again.

This is by far the most solitary poem in the sequence; it is only its context that declares it a love-poem at all. (True, the 'Unnamed Lady' has consigned her lover to God's service in the immediately preceding sonnet, but he doesn't seem to make much effort to contest his dismissal.) The sonnet accepts without reproach that an ageing woman can only expect frustration and silence. As so often in this sequence, Christina Rossetti gets her effects negatively, making words and images vivid by denying them, as with the line 'I will not bind fresh roses in my hair', which actually dramatizes the image of a faded woman inappropriately wreathed; similarly, the elegiac last line is dominated by the lost summer and singing which it renounces. The poem plays with tradition in a complex way that is not immediately apparent from its familiar materials. Roses, youth, summer and music are associated, conventionally enough, with the sexual flowering of woman as she is sung in courtly poems. But the 'silence' destined for age and the loss of beauty is not only that of actual loneliness but of exclusion from poetry, for this is the final sonnet in the sequence. This is partly because it is hardly worth her singing unless her lover is at least potentially capable of hearing her (as with sonnet I: 'the songs I sang / When life was sweet because you called them sweet'); it is also, more bitterly, because according to the conventions accepted by the poet, a woman does not belong in a poem, even her own, without 'youth and beauty'. Her love must remain 'pent up forlorn', without poetic expression, because in losing her looks she has lost the right to song. The sequence ends here; the stifled suffering has only begun.

I do not mean to argue (though it would be nice to think so) that Christina Rossetti, consciously encountering the sexual inequalities of courtly convention, is writing in 'Monna Innominata' a bitter commentary on the way a visionary like Petrarch makes a convenience of the beautiful female object of his passion. She is too deeply engaged with the very conventions whose limits her poems throw into relief for such criticism to exist as anything more than a subtext. Bitterness and anger are potentially present, but subordinated to a poetry of resignation to loss: that last line 'Silence of love that cannot sing again' comes over less as an enactment of frustration than as a melodious elegy. As the poet says in her preface, the point of the sonnets is to give the woman's side of the story, not to question its terms. And the Victorian sexual puritanism, which meant that she interpreted her heroine's chastity even more strictly than the mediaeval poets she was recalling, also meant that she defined the story's terms very narrowly indeed. For her, it is evidently unthinkable (though not impossible) that the heroine should desire anything more of the lover than his presence. If for Rossetti desire always exceeds any mortal satisfaction and the 'touch of hand in hand' is perpetually out of reach, isn't this in part at least determined by contemporary ideologies of female sexual purity, just as Millay's assertion that 'you shall be ... bowed and brought to bed with me' and her avowed relish for 'the way / your brown hair grows about your brow and cheek'[56] need to be read as an emancipated woman's defiance of those ideologies fifty years later?

These, however, are questions whose answers would explain some of the causes of the poems, not their textual effects. What does emerge from a close look at the sonnets of Edna St Vincent Millay and Christina Rossetti is that both wrote admirable though melancholy love poems without transforming or appropriating the Imaginary terms of the love-sonnet as it originated in masculine poetic tradition. Unlike the men, neither poet defines herself in relation to the ideal image constituted by the beloved of the opposite sex; such a reversal of sex-roles would be an impossibly violent shift for women working in a tradition which assigns them the role of mirror. And in any case, the male lovers imagined by both poets are very far from ideal: for Rossetti, he is either distant of forbidden or both; for Millay, he is cold and unsatisfactory; in both cases, he is finally unavailable. For neither poet is there any question of making White's demand for 'the whole of him, all the time',[57] even in fantasy. This is a sharp contrast to the mirror-poems, in which the beloved's presence (imagined by her gaze) guaranteed the man's identity, however chaste her response might be. The selfhood of both heroines is found not through either's relationship with the other, but in the finally solitary experience of loving excessively without adequate response. However striking their poetic achievements, we must look elsewhere for the creation of a specifically female Imaginary realm.

CHAPTER 5

'THE LIPS THAT NEVER LIE': FEMALE LANGUAGE AND IMAGINARY IDENTITY

> The Solemn – Torrid – Symbol
> The Lips that never lie –
> Whose hissing Corals part – and shut –
> And Cities – ooze away –
>
> (Emily Dickinson)
>
> . . . a whole new poetry beginning here.
> (Adrienne Rich)[1]

1 Women and Imaginary poetry

Imaginary identity is a concept originated by the psychoanalyst Jacques Lacan to describe the narcissistic relationship of doubles and reflections determining a crucial phase in the infantile acquisition of identity. This can conveniently be symbolized by the story, expounded and analysed in Lacan's influential essay 'Stade du Miroir', of the baby's captivation by its own mirror-image. But because in an Imaginary relationship the subject characteristically finds her or his own identity via an image granted by another, the term describes romantic love as well as archaic infantile fantasies. As I argue in Chapter 4 ('Two-Way Mirrors'), versions of these Imaginary processes can be found at work in traditional love-poems in which a masculine poet idealizes a figure (generally though not invariably that of a woman) into a mirroring muse who reflects back to him his own ideal image. This is a narcissistic form of representation, which denies true identity to its object in ways closely corresponding to those analysed by the French psycho-analyst Luce Irigaray (whose arguments are discussed in the first half of this chapter) as characteristic of masculine discourse in general. Irigaray argues that the real being of woman is denied by her transformation into a presence who must reflect to the (male) subject his own identity. The classic masculine love-poem is both structured and limited by this mirroring relationship, which defines the boundaries of its meaning, referring only indirectly to the world of social intercourse.

The obvious conclusion to be drawn from these arguments is that, being conventionally the means of reflecting masculine identities, women cannot readily reverse the process to create female subjectivities, and therefore cannot find it easy – or even possible – to produce poems in the Imaginary mode. The problem, however, is not so straightforward as this, since the correspondences between textual processes and the psychic histories of real women are indirect. Nor is the difficulty a simple matter of female narcissism being insufficient to produce the energies characteristic of Imaginary love-poems. It is, all the same, true that the sonnets by Millay and Rossetti which I analysed in Chapter 4 do not make their masculine Other into a muse or mirror resembling the idealized representations of women to be found in traditional masculine love-poems. Whereas the Imaginary poem enacts a fantasy of plenitude, of an Other who creates and grants one's own identity, these women poets begin with the premise that love is, for whatever reason, not fully returned, and satisfaction is not granted even in fantasy. (Elizabeth Barrett Browning's *Sonnets from the Portuguese*, which chronicle the poet's love affair from an uncertain and miserable beginning to its triumphant culmination in happy marriage, do of course constitute an obvious counter-example. But even here, though the story of these sonnets is their speaker's growth into trust and love, and though her lover's warmth and protection certainly enable her to find these capacities in herself, she does not discover her own identity through him. She grows through his care, which is not the same as defining herself through his fantasied presence.) Yet if an Imaginary mode of being could be discovered or glimpsed in women's poems, this would enable us to define or at least to imagine the elusive but fascinating idea of specifically female identity and meaning. And it is because the Imaginary realm is associated so strongly with the construction of human identity that it holds an important significance for feminists.

The idea of a female Imaginary mode of being has analogies with the notion of a women's tradition (discussed in Chapter 3) in being a female discourse which is not already 'there' like a buried object waiting to be dug up and labelled, but which is being created in the here and now by women poets and critics committed to feminism. The women's tradition is, in a sense, an intellectual counterpart to the existence of the committed feminists who are responsible for its construction. The idea of a female Imaginary is more elusive and ambiguous than that of a women's tradition, since the Imaginary mode of being is itself structured on fantasy; yet the way it raises questions of meaning and identity makes it particularly relevant to a feminist poetics. And it is a notion which needs to be considered in relation to poetry. This is partly because the construction of Imaginary relationships and identities demands the narrow intensity and perpetual present of the lyric 'I' of poetry or prose-poems (as with the Imaginary texts by Luce Irigaray and Monique Wittig discussed below on pp. 153–8). It is also because, as I have argued above in Chapter 1 (pp. 5–8), poetry emphasizes both the potency and the problematic nature of verbal meaning as no other form of writing does, by the way poems both interrogate and release the power of the words that constitute them.

It is partly through the contemplation and practice of women's poetry that the notion has emerged of a specifically female language which would articulate women's bodily experience, including physical love, childbirth and the memories of infantile sensuality. Mary Gentile argues that Adrienne Rich's poetry is the prototype of such a female-centred 'new language':

> Rich's language would evoke women's experience in all its multiplicity and undeniable immediacy in order to recognize it, understand it emotionally as well as intellectually, and affirm it simply because it is true and existent for the individual who experiences it . . . This new language and the mode of perception it implies, *are* the aims of her feminism. If I learn to express my experience as a woman in its entirety, in its physicality, in its complexity, without self-censorship, without employing externally imposed categories and evaluations, and with the conviction that my experience is valid, coherent and deserves attention, I will be speaking a new language.[2]

This manifesto is, as it stands, much too simple. The ambition to 'express my experience as a woman in its entirety', miraculously disentangled from history and from any discourse other than feminism ('without employing externally imposed categories') is a fantasy rather than an even remotely achievable goal. And the closeness of Rich's language to female physicality is imagined in naively literal terms when this critic claims to experience her poetry 'viscerally, with my body'[3] – a Romantic literal-mindedness that Rich herself shares when she writes how she was so overcome by her first reading of Judy Grahn's poem 'A Woman Is Talking to Death' that she collapsed with the symptoms of influenza:

'All that I could do . . . was lie down and sleep, let the flu run its course, and the knowledge that was accumulating in my life, the poem I had just read, go on circulating in my bloodstream'[4] – a response that oddly recalls A.E. Housman testing poetry by a physical response, namely whether or not it made his hairs bristle.

These radical feminist arguments for a poetry which is a language of authentic female being are a long way, politically and theoretically, from Irigarayan notions of a female language and identity. In particular, their insistence on the ideal of female identity as a seamless unity divides American radical feminists from those who use the Lacanian psychoanalytic notions of the Imaginary and the Symbolic. There is a split, as the influential 'Stade du Miroir' essay argues, between the baby's assumption of an ideal identity via an image granted by its mother, and the physical experience of being held by her as it looks in the mirror; the Imaginary mode of being is both structured by and denies that split. In a similar though not identical way, there is always in speech a split between the self which says 'I' and the word 'I' that is spoken. I do not think that radical feminists like Rich or her critic Gentile would concede that such splitting is necessary to the existence of meaning and identity. On the contrary, their ideal is to reintegrate inner divisions; whereas a post-Lacanian like Irigaray would agree that such splitting is fundamental both to the existence of meaning in general and to the conception of the Imaginary mode of being in particular, although she would reformulate this in less visual and more tactile metaphors than Lacan does.[5]

But despite these real differences of thought, the ways in which both kinds of feminist insist on the significance of a new – or repressed – women's language, mark this concern both as overtly political and as important for feminist critics to think about. The idea of a female Imaginary identity is the best way that I know of approaching these ideals and possibilities of specifically female meaning. For as we shall see when we examine Luce Irigaray's ideas and arguments closely, to formulate a female identity is really a way of understanding the problems and possibilities of women in language.

2 Irigaray and the Imaginary

Luce Irigaray has theorized women's identity and sexuality through a critique of language, philosophy and psycho-analysis so subtle and difficult as to be impossible to summarize without distortion. To put this critique briefly (as, however great the risk of oversimplifying it, is necessary): in the essays collected in *Speculum, de l'autre femme* (1974) and *Ce Sexe qui n'en est pas un* (1977), she analyses the underlying structures of thought in Freud, Plato and Hegel, arguing that these men's intellectual systems are based on oppositions in which the second term is understood as a devalued opposite to the first; within such definitions, whether overt or covert, woman gets assimilated to the negative pole – other, irrational, material: that is, to being thought of as the matter whose mirroring existence makes possible the light of masculine Reason. In other words, Irigaray's project of analysing such interdependent oppositions as identity/difference or male/female, is essentially deconstructive. As Carolyn Burke has written of deconstruction, 'the aim is not to neutralize the oppositional structure, but rather, to demonstrate the inequality of the terms locked into opposition. In such a structure, according to Derrida, "One of the two terms controls the other ... holds the superior position. To deconstruct the opposition is first to overthrow (*renverser*) the hierarchy." However the task is not yet complete: "in the next phase of deconstruction, this reversal must be displaced, and the 'winning' term used without giving it the winning status that its opposite once possessed." [6] In a recent interview, Irigaray has confirmed her commitment to deconstructive practice:

> I think it is necessary to act in two ways. First, to criticise the existing system, and that is perhaps what is pardoned the least, because people are not going to accept that you might put in question a theoretical system . . . We have to reject all the great systems of opposition on which our culture is constructed. Reject, for instance, the oppositions: fiction/truth, sensible/intelligible, empirical/transcendental, materialist/idealist. All these opposing pairs function as an exploitation and a negation at the beginning and of a certain mode of connection between the body and the word for which we have paid everything.[7]

The depth and energy of Luce Irigaray's critical and polemic engagement with the monuments of patriarchal philosophy whose terms she analyses in *Speculum* has not always been understood in discussions of her work, nor has the interdependence between her notions of female language and her project of deconstruction. Her multi-punning and highly allusive style, as well as the intrinsic difficulty of her arguments, make for exhausting reading; furthermore, until *Speculum* and *Ce Sexe qui n'en est pas un* became available in English as *Speculum of the Other Woman* and *The Sex Which Is Not One* in 1985, her work was mainly represented in translation by a handful of comparatively approachable but not entirely character-istic texts, all concerned specifically with female identity.[8] Because her work of deconstruction has not been widely available in English until now, she has often been typed – and dismissed – as an exponent of naively essentialist fem-inism, who valorizes a stereotyped description of Woman as an inarticulate being whose buried 'language' expresses only the biological materiality of her body.[9] Irigaray's arguments for female identity and language are, as the following summary shows, much more subtle than that.

The essays in *Speculum* and *Ce Sexe qui n'en est pas un*
argue that the available, masculine-determined forms of
representation victimize women by endowing us with a
language incapable of articulating our meanings and thus
alienating us from our psychic identities. We are, Irigaray
says, alienated from our being through existing in
language only as a negative, a 'hole', and through the
psychic processes, determined in part by language,
whereby we acquire our identities as women. (In her
analysis, men are also affected painfully by the contradictions in the means of representation available in our
culture, *but* since the phallus is the 'privileged signifier',
they retain the masculine privilege of symbolizing what is
positive and visible. There are also, of course, the real-life
power and privilege enjoyed by men, but Irigaray's
argument is directed primarily at the disabling effects of
representation.) When Freud and Lacan analysed the
relation between the human psyche and language, their
own work reproduced this linguistic denial of the realities
of female language and experience, not because their
arguments are mistaken (Irigaray endorses them, as far as
they go), but because both men failed to press them far
enough to question their own intellectual systems. Their
thought, assumptions and language all manifest patriarchy's blind spot to women as anything but the negative
of the masculine.[10] The work of these men reduplicated
the definition of woman in terms of maternity which is
enforced by the unconscious fantasies that govern human
lives, and which they themselves analysed and codified.
Outside of this alienating fantasy of herself as mother,
woman's 'otherness' is felt as a frightful abyss of
nothingness that negates definition:

> The mother perhaps signifies only a dumb soil, a hardly
> figurable mystery, but at least she is *full*. Certainly you
> find there opacity and resistance, even the aversion of
> matter, the horror of blood, the ambivalence of milk,
> the menacing traces of the paternal phallus and even

the hole you leave behind yourself in coming into the world. But she – at least – is not nothing. She is not that empty(ness of) Woman. That annihilation of representation, that limit of all representation (of the self) as present . . . He [man] needs, then, to know her in order to enclose her in his system. Not that of the woman, from whom he can only protect himself by (re)constituting her as mother or by opposing to her . . . the saving disguise of a language which has already translated her very differences into fetishes.[11]

In the fantasy that underpins masculine discourse, then, woman has to be cast in the role of monstrous Kleinian mother lest worse befall. That is: lest man risk the annihilation of his meanings by the admission of her (to him) alien identity. But the maternal role holds another, greater problem for women, which is also an aspect of the lack of meaning which we suffer: namely, the little girl's alienation from her mother. Irigaray has said in an interview:

Everything happens as though there were a necessary break between the earliest investments, the earliest desires, the first narcissism of a little girl and those of a 'normal' adult woman. In the place of those who would be in a position of continuity with her pre-history she has imposed on her a language, fantasms, a desire which does not 'belong' to her and which establishes a break with her auto-eroticism.[12]

If women are to find their own identity and meaning, it is necessary to repossess out primitive love for the mother: the baby's first, pre-Oedipal bond. In other words, we need to repossess our identities through reclaiming as women our lost Imaginary state. But at present we are still trapped in exile. According to Irigaray:

The important thing is to try to understand how the mother could change in the acutal system. But it is impossible; she cannot change. One might as well believe in Santa Claus. What can we do? Condemn her a little more? Freud says that our culture is built upon a parricide. More fundamentally, our culture is built upon the matricide of the mother/lover – not of the woman as reproducer but of the woman as a lover, as a creator who has a specific desire and who fights for that desire . . . If the mother is the alienator, it is because she has no identity as a woman. And this effectively plunges the mother and the little girl in the same nothingness. But the problem is neither to accuse the mother nor to say that it is the father who comes to liberate the little girl. The mother has to find her identity as a woman, and from that point she could be able to give an identity to her daughter. But this is the key point to which our system is most blind.[13]

In the well-known poem 'Transcendental Etude', Adrienne Rich contemplates the primordial love between girl-child and mother in terms which suggest Irigaray's:

Birth stripped our birth-right from us,
tore us from a woman, from ourselves . . .
and the whole chorus throbbing at our ears
like midges, told us nothing . . .

Only: that it is unnatural,
that homesickness for a woman, for ourselves,
for that acute joy at the shadow her head or arms
cast on a wall, her heavy or slender
thighs on which we lay, flesh against flesh,
eyes steady on the face of love; smell of her milk,
    her sweat,
terror of her disappearance, all fused in this hunger
for the element they have called most dangerous[14]

Rich's vivid representation of infantile sensuality at once appeals to our nostalgia and seems to return us to the lost love which she evokes, while her poignant lyricism emphasizes the ironic intention of the phrase 'it is unnatural'. For Rich, love between women is the most natural thing in the world. Yet this also marks a difference between herself and Irigaray. Rich's poem articulates a lesbian-feminist analysis of woman's psychology (not shared by Irigaray), which understands women's psychic history in terms of a fall from this state of sensual unity with the mother into the alienating condition of compulsory heterosexuality.[15] She does not assent to the psychoanalytic concept of *repression*, which in Irigaray's more pessimistic thinking is crucially significant in constituting female identity. A quite different poem representing the processes of repression in the psyche, which can also help to interpret Irigaray's arguments, is W.H. Auden's early 'The Question'. Although this poem concerns a masculine psyche (an Oedipal victim lost in his own evasions), it is usefully relevant to Irigaray's analysis of repression in identity. In 'The Question', the subject's mind is a desert of lost memory where

> ... ghosts must do again
> What gives them pain.

> Cowardice cries
> For windy skies,
> Coldness for water,
> Obedience for a master.[16]

The subject in this poem is capable only of alienated desire. He cannot imagine and therefore does not want release from his own imprisoned condition. Instead, he desires the images which will represent his mind's repression and defeat: 'cowardice cries / For windy skies' — (that is, for the image of its own flight). As with Irigaray, there is a dream of dissolving the bonds of repression in a return to and repossession of the mother:

> Can love remember
> The question and the answer,
> For love recover
> What has been dark and rich and warm all over?[17]

But there is no guarantee, for either the poem or the psychoanalyst, that the answer to these questions will be 'yes'; especially as in Irigaray's thought the relation between mother and daughter is, as the passage from the interview quoted above suggests, less blissful than troubles. In her small book *Et l'une ne bouge sans l'autre* ('And the One Doesn't Stir Without the Other'), a prose-poem spoken in fantasy by a daughter to her mother, repulsion is expressed for the fleshiness and physical intimacy which in Rich's poem represent desire:

> You've gone again. Once more you're assimilated into nourishment. We've again disappeared into this act of eating each other. Hardly do I glimpse you and walk towards you, when you metamorphose into a baby nurse. Again you want to fill my mouth, my belly, to make yourself into a plenitude for mouth and belly. To let nothing pass between us but blood, milk, honey and meat . . . Will there never be love between us other than this filling up of holes? To close off and seal up everything that could happen between us, indefinitely, is that your only desire? To reduce us to consuming and being consumed, is that your only need?[18]

For Irigaray, then, the work of discovering and defining woman's identity is not only a matter of rediscovering our early, pre-Oedipal attachment to the mother. It is also (as my phrase 'the mother' rather than 'our mothers' indicates), a work of representation, of finding new psychoanalytical models and myths to articulate what is at present indefinable: that is, the existence of women in language whose terms currently efface female being. At this stage of the argument, such language appears like a closed system which we cannot alter because we are unable to say which came first, the linguistically alienated chicken or the emotionally addled egg.

3 Identity and language

> She would not say of one single person in the world now that they were this or they were that.
>
> (Virginia Woolf)[19]

Contradiction makes change possible. For Irigaray, woman is indefinable in existing language, the spanner in the works, the defeat of representation,[20] while at the same time she, or rather the metaphors that conceal her, is indispensable to its workings. The symbolic system which she as it were props up is predominantly a visual one in which her function is to make it possible for man to view the ideal image of his own identity. *Speculum* is, as its title suggests, full of mirror-imagery; and Irigaray's account of how woman makes masculine meaning and symbolization possible strongly recalls Frederick Goldin's exposition in *The Mirror of Narcissus*, discussed in Chapter 4 (pp. 109–12), of the ways in which the 'mirror-poems' show how the high-minded illusions of romantic love are made possible by the poet defining his lady as a mirror reflecting 'what she does not truly possess'[21] that is, the ideal to which he aspires. This idealization by the poet (as Goldin's discussion does *not* say, whereas Irigaray's analysis of the same material does, repeatedly) effaces the identity and thought of the lady: what is important is the meaning she holds for *him*. Irigaray universalizes this process, finding it at work in the structures of significant difference that constitute language. As she writes in a characteristically obscure but suggestive passage: 'Woman still remains this nothing-at-all, this totality of nothingness (*ce tout du rien, rien du tout*) where each masculine unity (*un*) comes to look for what will replenish the resemblance to self, (as it were) to sameness. Thus she is displaced, but it is never quite she who is displaced. She cannot herself unsettle the displacement/disturb the ownership* of the place which she constitutes for the (male) subject, and to which no once-for-all value can be assigned for fear that he (the subject) would get his assets unalterably frozen.'[22] The point of these economic metaphors is that it is the repression of her meaning that makes his thought possible. But woman's being is not itself a mystery, only impossible to define in a masculine linguistic system informed by high valuation of unity, solidity and visibility, and equating identity with sameness.[23] This language of false clarity cannot define women, let alone articulate their selves. Hence the incomprehensibility of women, proverbially *varium et mutabile semper* ('various and always changing'):

'She' is indefinitely other in herself. This is undoubtedly the reason she is called temperamental, incomprehensible, perturbed, capricious – not to mention her language in which 'she' goes off in all directions and in which 'he' is unable to discern the coherence of any meaning. Contradictory words seem a little crazy to the logic of reason, and inaudible to him who listens with ready-made grids, a code prepared in advance.[24]

Woman's identity and discourse need to be understood as multiple and fluid; Irigaray symbolizes the specificity of women's being and sexuality in what has become the well-known metaphor of labia which symbolize unity in plurality:

---

*There is an untranslatable pun here in Irigaray's phrase 'ce tenant (du) lieu' meaning both 'this displacement' (ce tenant lieu) and 'this ownership' (ce tenant de lieu) – a characteristic instance of her contradictory style.

When one says or believes that this sex is a 'hole', it is a way of indicating that it cannot represent itself in either the dominant discourse or 'imaginary'. Thus I have tried to find out what the specific modes of functioning of the female sex and 'imaginary' could be . . . I'm trying to say that the female sex would be, above all, made up of 'two lips'. These two lips of the female sex make it once and for all a return to unity, because they are always at least two, and one can never determine of these two, which is one, which is the other: they are continually interchanging. They are neither identifiable nor separable from one another . . . it is the *touch* which for the female sex seems to me primordial; these *two lips* are always joined in an embrace.[25]

This metaphor of 'two lips' is *not* a definition of women's identity in biological terms: the statement that they are 'continually interchanging' must make it clear that Irigaray is not talking about literal biology. She is, rather, offering the metaphor as a means of representation, creating a possible vocabulary for the female imagination other than the Freudian opposition 'phallic/castrated'. In its context of language-discussion, the metaphor of 'two lips' is evidently a counter-proposal to the psychoanalytic association of the right to speech with possession of the phallus;[26] suggesting as the oral image does not exactly speech, but the capacity for articulation; it thus connotes a female subjectivity potentially creating its own meanings. It would seem that this redefinition of female identity can be accurately summed up in the verse from Emily Dickinson quoted as epigraph to this chapter:

> The Solemn – Torrid – Symbol
> The Lips that never lie
> Whose hissing Corals part – and shut –
> And Cities – ooze away –[27]

This reads almost like a prophetic allegory of female

language, especially if one accepts – as, it must be said, Irigaray does not – that anger as well as alienation characterize female identity: a vision of the annihilation of a constricting system, where the 'lips that never lie' utter their flow of language (the heat of the molten lava symbolizing dammed-up rage) and the 'cities' of masculine reason are not just submerged but 'ooze' into its scalding stickiness. The parallel between the figurative flows of lava and language is strengthened by Irigaray's frequent insistence in *Ce Sexe qui n'en est pas un*[28] on the association between femaleness and liquidity which can seem shapelessness, the fluidity of women's identity, and the need to accept the changeable movements of liquids as appropriate metaphors for female discourse: 'Woman never speaks evenly. What she utters is flowing, fluctuating. *Deceptive* ["*flouant*", punning on "fluent"]. And you cannot hear her, except by losing the "right" and "literal" meaning.'[29] It is also possible, via this association of femaleness with fluidity, to link the flow of lava with that of blood and perhaps menstruation, a connection which is again reinforced by the passage in Irigaray's 'Quand nos lèvres se parlent' ('When Our Lips Speak Together') which puns on the sounds of '*sang*' (blood) and '*sens*' (meaning, sense) to create an analogy between female sexuality and language:

> Wait. My blood is coming back from their senses. It's getting warmer inside us, between us. Their words are becoming empty, bloodless, dead skins. While our lips are becoming red again. They're stirring, they're moving, they want to speak.[30]

These reddening lips and Dickinson's 'hissing Corals' are apparently equivalent metaphors for female self-expression – appropriately enough, if volcanoes are, as Adrienne Rich has written, 'eternally and visibly female'.[31] It is no wonder that Irigaray's theoretical work has been received with hostility, if it threatens the cities of logocentrism with such a blazing eruption.

But though this feminist reading of the Dickinson verse does work, the parallel with Irigaray is finally misleading. The volcano will not really do as a symbol for Irigaray's conception of female identity and language: no spatial metaphor will, since it is bound to suggest that what is repressed is merely *sub*-conscious: underneath, waiting to boil up one day and overwhelm everything. This comparatively straightforward essentialist allegory, in which women's language is simply our damned-up unspoken meanings, is much closer to the feminism of *The Madwoman in the Attic* than to Irigaray's notions of women's otherness and undependability; in her thinking, *no* definition of woman is acceptable as complete or final, not even her own. Women are both inside and outside discourse,[32] which has no space for what is specifically female: 'Must the multiple nature of female desire and language be understood as the fragmentary, scattered remains of a raped or denied sexuality? This is not an easy question to answer. The rejection, the exclusion of a female imaginary undoubtedly places woman in a position where she can experience herself only fragmentarily as waste or excess in the little structured margins of the dominant ideology, this mirror entrusted by the (masculine) 'subject' with the task of reflecting and redoubling himself.'[33] But though Irigaray is evasive in answering her own question, it is clear that she does think that plurality and indefiniteness are important characteristics of female identity. She has written in a much-criticized passage of the essay 'Ce Sexe qui n'en est pas un':

It is therefore useless to trap women into giving an exact definition of what they mean, to make them repeat (themselves) so that meaning will be clear. They are already elsewhere than in this discursive machinery. They have turned back within themselves . . . They do not experience the same interiority that you (men) do and which you perhaps mistakenly presume they share. 'Within themselves' means in the *privacy of this silent, multiple, diffusive tact*. If you ask them insistently what they are thinking about, they can only reply: nothing. Everything.[34]

The socialist feminist Monique Plaza has made a damaging criticism of this passage, accusing Irigaray of reducing women to idiotically inarticulate versions of the Eternal Feminine.[35] This is not, however, a just criticism. Irigaray is insisting (in terms which are, admittedly, extremely irritating to feminists who value clarity of exposition) that anyone who would understand female speech and writing must bring to it a capacity for multiple interpretation and a sensitivity to its plurality of meanings. The best gloss on the assertion of woman's indefiniteness quoted above is 'Quand nos lèvres se parlent' ('When Our Lips Speak Together'), the lyrical epilogue to *Ce Sexe qui n'en est pas un*, especially the passage when one of the lovers says tenderly, 'What do you want to say? Nothing. Everything. Yes. Be patient. You will say it all. Begin with what you feel, here, right away.'[36]

Irigaray's insistence on women's fluidity and plurality of speech is, then, as much a prescription for the reader's response as a description of female identity; it describes an approach as well as the thing approached. Correspondingly, her discursive method very often consists in offering and at the same time withdrawing a list of definitions of the feminine, none of which quite fits. She often sounds much less like an authority on language than like the baffling woman in Eliot's poem:

> 'That is not what I meant, at all.
> That is not it, at all.'[37]

4 Textual erotics: Irigaray and Wittig

When I see you talking nearby, my heart thuds, my
tongue is held in silence, and a subtle fire runs under
my skin, I see nothing and my hearing is confused,
sweat runs down me, shuddering seizes me all over, I
am greener than grass, and I seem little short of death.
(Sappho)[38]

Although for Irigaray female identity and language are
possibilities rather than actualities, to be glimpsed and
evoked, not described, she has produced one text, 'Quand
nos lèvres se parlent' ('When Our Lips Speak Together'),
which is specifically concerned with a female Imaginary
world constituted by a pair of lovers. Like Monique
Wittig's *The Lesbian Body*, discussed below, this text is
written in punning, experimental, multi-layered prose. *It*
is a conscious attempt to write the Imaginary:

I love you, childhood. I love you, who are not my
mother (sorry, mother, I prefer a woman to you) nor
sister. Neither daughter nor son. I love you – and there
where I love you, the filiations of the fathers and their
desire for reflections of men don't matter. And their
genealogical institutions – neither husband nor wife.
No personality, role or function for their reproductive
laws. I love you: your body, there, here, now. I/you
touch you/me, it's enough for us to know ourselves
alive . . .
   Are we unsatisfied? Yes, if that means we are never
finished. If our pleasure is to move ourselves, to be
moved, endlessly. Always in movement; openness is not
exhausted nor satiated.[39]

The gentle anarchy of this (auto)erotic prose poem (for it
is not certain whether two lovers are 'present' here) is
strengthened by its fluid ambiguities; not only do the
lovers escape from social definition, but it is impossible to

say which of them is speaking at any one moment. This is fantasy, certainly, but not escapist so much as, literally, utopian. It represents the speech of and between women, enacted in a linguistic 'nowhere': that is, the performative text read and created in the reader's mind. The 'Quand' of the title locates the text in a temporal 'altogether elsewhere'; this, it suggests, is how language could be imagined 'when our lips speak together', but the time clause trails off and the sentence is unfinished . . .

It is tempting to complete that unfinished sentence with 'elles disent' ('the women say'), the phrase constantly reiterated in Monique Wittig's *Les Gúerillères*. The text by Wittig which resembles Irigaray in writing the female Imaginary is however *Le Corps lesbien* (1973, translated as *The Lesbian Body*, 1976), which also creates a utopian world of female-centred meaning, inhabited entirely by women and full of female or feminized legends. As Helène Wenzel has pointed out, each of Wittig's fictions has presented a kind of linguistic utopia: 'In Wittig's sex-segregated worlds, where the question of sex differences and categories is irrelevant, women may provisionally create women who constitute themselves as speaking/naming subjects of discourse.'[40] The speaker of *The Lesbian Body* sets sail for the black and gold islands of a lesbian archipelago[41] whose guardian genius is the poet Sappho. This is the background for the two (unnamed) lovers *j/e* and *tu*, whose mergings and separations constitute the narrative of the book, so far as it has one: it consists formally of a series of present-tense monologues spoken by *j/e* to *tu*, giving the effect of a cycle of prose-poems. Though this resembles Irigaray's much shorter text in creating a female world consisting almost entirely of self and other, Wittig is much more violent and experimental. She insists like Irigaray that existing language is alien to women's identities, and she dramatizes this by typographically splitting the '*je*' who speaks, making her a literally divided subject. As she writes in the preface:

The 'I' (*je*) who speaks is alien to her writing at every word because this 'I' (*je*) uses a language alien to her; this 'I' (*je*) cannot be *un* ecrivain [i.e. she has to make herself inappropriately masculine to denote herself as writer – JM] . . . J/e is the symbol of the lived, rending experience which is m/y writing, of this cutting in two which is the exercise of a language which does not constitute m/e as subject.[42]

Less obviously transgressive, and perhaps less effective, is Wittig's way of claiming meaning as both feminized and as problematic for women by appropriating traditional legends to her women's utopia, using such devices as lists of heroines, references to 'Ulyssea', 'Zeyna and Ganymedea', 'Achillea, she who loved Patroclea',[43] and so on. This is tricky as a method of dramatizing the contradictions between women's consciousness and patriarchal inheritance, because unless readers have enough classical education to pick up Wittig's references, the specific tensions between traditional mythology and lesbian-feminist meaning disappear, leaving the text haunted by the names of numinous but indistinct heroines. This leaching of their own significance from the classical legends alluded to tends to happen as one reads anyway: Wittig's lovers faint or die and then come to life so often that whether they do so by way of 'you singing with victorious voice the joy of m/y recovery . . . you drag m/e to the surface of the earth where the sun is visible'[44] or re-enact the suffering of 'Christa',[45] one is less aware of the woman speaker as a 'thief of language'[46] stealing the myths of Orpheus or of the Crucifixion than of the endlessly repeated death-into-life.[47] These repeated extremities of bodily experience also, more straightforwardly, recall the Sappho poem quoted as epigraph to this section (p. 153). For *The Lesbian Body* is a violently physical book: as Helène Wenzel puts, '*j/e* and *tu* literally tear each other apart and put each other together again . . . They recreate themselves through cellular interpenetration, eclipsing simple penetration, in which desire for self and other is whetted and sated infinitely.'[48] This is a typically outrageous passage:

I have access to your glottis and your larynx red with blood voice stifled. I reach your trachea, I embed myself as far as your left lung, there m/y so delicate one I place m/y two hands on the pale pink bland mass, touched it unfolds somewhat, it moves fanwise, my knees flex, I gather into my mouth your entire reserves of air. Mixed with it are traces of smoke, odours of herbs, the scent of flowers, irises it seems to m/e, the lung begins to beat, it gives a jump while tears flow from your wide-open eyes, you trap m/y mouth like a cupping-glass on the sticky mass of your lung, large soft sticky fragments insert themselves between m/y lips, shape themselves to m/y palate, the entire mass is engulfed in m/y open mouth, m/y tongue is caught in an indescribable glue, a jelly descends towards m/y glottis I choke and you choke without a cry, at this moment m/y most pleasing of all women it is impossible to conceive a more magistral a more inevitable coupling.[49]

This verbal eroticism is so violently physical as to prevent the book from being in any straightforward sense a pleasurable text. But though far more extreme than anything in Irigaray, Wittig's utopian fantasy is arguably a logical outcome of the psychoanalyst's insistence on the need to make available a female Imaginary realm (though I do not know whether this is a conscious development of the other's theories on Wittig's part). For if this Imaginary realm or mode of being is to be incarnated in any specifically woman-centred relationships, the participants must be either the original Imaginary dyad of mother-and-baby, or lesbian lovers. *The Lesbian Body*, intentionally or not, includes both, precisely because its representation of self-and-others engages with the earliest and most primitive Imaginary fantasies. In particular, the oral sadism (a psychoanalytic term *not* a moral criticism) which Melanie Klein identified as characteristic of primitive infantile eroticism is a very marked feature of its monologues, as in that quoted above. The book is full of the passion to possess and devour, of anxiety (to use an Irigayan pun) at the (m)other's possible absence which makes *j/e* cry and collapse in a faint,[50] and of fantasies of omnipotence, manifested in the power to revive the dead. The body of *tu* appears as a 'good breast' torn to pieces, devoured, vomited and reabsorbed. The world of the lovers' dyad is, consonantly with this primitive love, basically a-social despite the frequent presence of groups or crowds of other women. Because their Imaginary relationship belongs to the most archaic, pre-Oedipal emotional structures, there is no family present (not even to be negated, as in the Irigaray passage quoted above, p. 153), and above all, no paternal prohibition. This means that *j/e*'s access to and enjoyment of the (m)other's body can be imagined as total. Hence the repetitiveness of the book, whose monologues relate union and recognition, followed by rejection and separation, followed by repeated mergings, sunderings and mergings in an endlessly repeated present. And this is entirely appropriate, since developed narrative does not belong to Imaginary states.[51] On the other hand, because there is no question of gender in this mode of being, there is no reason why this violent pre-Oedipal realm inhabited by *j/e* and *tu* should be specifically female. It can indeed be argued that, because the archaic energies engaged by Imaginary fantasies and anxieties derive from a mode of being in which the presence or absence of the other is the dominant feature, rather than the desires originating from the castration complex and the idea of sexual difference, Imaginary writing, far from transcending problems of gender, simply evades them. It would, of course, be absurd to call Wittig's outrageously women-centred textual erotics evasive; but certainly the Imaginary dyad of self-and-other, beyond all constraints of family or social practice, which structures her text as well as Irigaray's, is utopian in the sense of being impossible to place in reality. How far these erotic utopias can be effective as lights by which to read the work of women poets can best be determined by applying these concepts to poems.

5 Ambiguity and contradiction: Warner, Rich and Dickinson

'He was part of my dream, of course – but then I was part of his dream, too!'[52]
(Lewis Carroll, *Through the Looking-Glass*)

A love-poem which comes close to creating a female Imaginary identity is Sylvia Townsend Warner's 'Drawing you, heavy with sleep to lie closer'. Because this is little known, it needs quoting in full:

Drawing you, heavy with sleep to lie closer
Staying your poppy head upon my shoulder
    It was as though I pulled the glide
    Of a full river to my side.

Heavy with sleep and with sleep pliable,
You rolled at a touch towards me. Your arm fell
    Across me as a river throws
    An arm of flood across meadows.

And as the careless water its mirroring sanction
Grants to him at the river's brim long stationed,
    Long drowned in thought, that yet he lives,
    Since in that mirroring tide he moves,

Your body lying by mine to mine responded,
Your hair stirred on my mouth, my image was dandled

> Deep in your sleep that flowed unstained
> On from the image entertained.[53]

This representation of the sleeper's unconscious response as a 'mirroring tide' in which the 'I' knows herself, and particularly its deployment of images of flowing and liquidity, which Luce Irigaray identifies as specifically characteristic of female sexuality, evidently suggests that an Imaginary relationship is being created here, especially since both lovers are women,[54] which is close to that articulated in 'When our lips speak together,' discussed above (p. 153). Although traditional in form and apparently simple enough on a first reading – the 'I' of the text is not, for instance, interchangeable between the lovers, as in Irigaray's prose-poem – the poem nevertheless plays with identity, mobility and reflection in comparably complex ways. The image offered of the person contemplating his own image in the still river can be readily identified with the tableau of the child enchanted by its own image which Lacan analyses in the essay 'The Mirror-Phase'; indeed, 'my image was dandled' is a phrase in which an impossibly articulate baby might describe the icon of itself and mother framed in the mirror, which that essay sets up as myth or model of identity. But touch is even more important than sight in this poem: the reflecting water is a metaphor for physical closeness, so that it is the embrace where 'Your body lying by mine to mine responded' that confers identity on the 'I'. The sleeper deep in her dream (which is of course illusion, as all the dreams are), nevertheless 'entertains' an image which coincides perfectly with the truth. This interplay between the speaker's contemplative awareness and her lover's caressive, unconscious but not unthinking response, evokes an Irigarayan sense of unity in division. As in that dual monologue, the lovers are alone, equal, flowing, untroubled by roles of mother, daughter, sister; there is even a hint of interchanging identities in the image of the person who knows he lives, 'Since in that mirroring tide he moves' — is it he who moves, or the current? At the same time the lover is not reduced to being a means of reflection: the materiality of the sleeper's body, breathing and stirring, which 'rolled . . . towards me' like the full river of the simile, is insisted on. The sleeper, who can be encountered but not possessed, and whose mind is present but hidden, eludes as well as meets the 'I', who can only trust that her own dream is shared, never prove it.

But the poem is not a straightforwardly fluent analogy to Irigaray's ideal lovers. The simile of the watcher by the river, rich in connotations of liquidity, identity and reflection though it is, poses a distinct problem for the critic who wants to read the poem as an enclave of woman-centred meaning, articulating a sexual identity through a female language of fluid metaphor. The difficulty lies in the small but recalcitrant point that this contemplative gazer, 'him at the river's brim', is designated as masculine. The fact is of course easy enough to explain. The date of the poem's composition, 1935,[55] long pre-dates the existence of a feminist critique of language-uses, so that 'he' and 'him' should be construed in this poem as meaning 'anybody'; alternatively, it can be argued that the introduction of the masculine pronoun evaded any possible censorship of the poem's lesbian eroticism. The trouble is that these explanations confirm rather than counter the real difficulty, which is that the poem does *not* fully transcend the assumptions — that 'he' can denote all humanity, or that desire is always heterosexual — which are encoded in the language-conventions it is using. However good a poem it is — and I hope my analysis makes clear how much I admire it — 'Drawing you, heavy with sleep' cannot be claimed as an instance of female discourse existing outside the constraints of history; and perhaps the claim that any text can really do so is unrealistic.

Adrienne Rich's sequence 'Twenty-One Love Poems', addressed to an unknown lover, certainly do not set out to make such a separation from history: especially at the idyllic beginning of the sequence, they are full of the 'dailiness of life' – cinemas, sacks of groceries, New York geography, books in a study. The poem indicates by these details of ordinary life that the lovers do not inhabit an ideal world:

> two women together is a work
> nothing in civilization has made simple,
> two people together is a work
> heroic in its ordinariness,
> the slow-picked, halting traverse of a pitch
> where the fiercest attention becomes routine –
> look at the faces of those who have chosen it.
>
> (Poem XIX)*

Roads, streets, beaches and Manhattan exist in the poems mainly as settings, however: as usual in love-poems, the only presences are the 'I' and the lover. But although the sequence is plainly autobiographical, and even self-analytic, the poet does not use the other as a defining presence who enables her to discover her own identity. Certainly, Rich has written some brilliant first-person poems which articulate an identity in relation to an alter ego, notably 'The Mirror in Which Two Are Seen as One' and 'Diving into the Wreck',[56] but these love-poems are not among them. Rich's feminist commitment, which is connected to her evident respect for the other's identity as a woman, seems actually to lead her in the opposite direction, to a refusal to use the other to structure her own self-explorations:

---

* As with the sonnet sequences discussed in Chapter 4, I am identifying individual poems by their numerals in the published sequence.

Your silence today is a pond where drowned things live
I want to see raised dripping and brought into the sun.
It's not my own face I see there, but other faces,
even your own face at another age.

. . . .

           . . . Even the silt and pebbles of the bottom
deserve their recognition.

(Poem IX)

The 'I' neither makes her lover into a consciousness
reflecting her own self nor claims to speak on her behalf;
on the contrary, she worries lest the inevitable gap
between the text she produces and her lived, shared
experience, may make her risk reducing her lover to a
prop in her own poems' linguistic drama:

What kind of beast would turn its life into words?
What atonement is this all about?
– and yet, writing words like these, I'm also living.
Is all this close to the wolverines' howled signals,
that modulated cantata of the wild?
Or, when away from you I try to create you in words,
am I simply using you, like a river or a war?

(Poem VII)

Poem XX, the only one in the sequence which does seem
to make the lover into a mirror-opposite (and which,
incidentally, uses the water-imagery which for Rich, as
for many women poets, symbolizes the depths of the
psyche), also records a failure. The 'I', alone in Manhattan,
is looking into the Hudson river at midnight:

polluted water reflecting even
sometimes the moon
and I discern a woman
I loved, drowning in secrets, fear wound round
   her throat,
choking her like hair. And this is she

with whom I tried to speak, whose hurt, expressive
    head
turning aside from pain, is dragged down deeper
where it cannot hear me
and soon I shall know I was talking to my own
    soul.

Like many of Rich's best poems, this purports to re-create
experience straightforwardly, but actually creates a fable.
The drowned woman can certainly be identified with the
lover addressed in the poems, but not literally, any more
than 'Diving into the Wreck' narrates an actual experience
of skin-diving. The woman who drowns in silence is, I
think, to be construed as the victim of her own evasion,
as if the silence (which was 'a pond where drowned
things live' in poem IX) had enlarged itself into a choking
river of 'polluted water'. In 'Women and Honor: Some
Notes on Lying', produced during the same period as the
love-poems,[57] Rich explores the destructive effects of
such evasions:

Lying is done with words, and also with silence.
    The woman who tells lies in her personal relationships
may not plan or invent her lying. She may not even
think of what she is doing in a calculated way.[58]

The speechlessness of the drowning woman is 'fear
wound round her throat / choking her like hair': the
poem articulates in this image the insight that 'Lying is
done . . . with silence'. It has been suggested that the
silence between the two women transcends words, so that
the last line, 'and soon I shall know I was talking to my
own soul', evokes a unity by which 'in a 'deeper',
repressed sense, the two women meet and merge'.[59] This
is optimistic. The speaker discovers that she is talking to
herself – and perhaps has only ever talked to herself –
because the other is too frightened or cowardly ('turning

aside from pain') to hear her words. Identification is implied, but of an ominous kind, as if, having become sucked into the other's 'fear of the void',[60] she has become a liar by silence too. Again, 'Women and Honor' is a useful gloss:

> Why do we feel slightly crazy when we realize we have been lied to in a relationship?
> . . . When we discover that someone we trusted can no longer be trusted, it forces us to re-examine the universe, to question the whole concept of trust. For awhile, we are thrust back onto some bleak, jutting ledge, in a dark pierced by sheets of fire, swept by sheets of rain, in a world before kinship, or naming, or tenderness exist; we are brought close to formlessness.[61]

It is no accident, either, that a poem about lying and alienation should end with the poet talking to 'my own soul': her respect for the other woman's identity, which in earlier poems led her to question the act of writing them ('when . . . I try to create you in words / am I simply using you?' – VII), does not survive what seems like a defeat by the other's failure to acknowledge the painful truth. For the sequence itself reads like the intermittent diary of a love-affair which passes its peak about two-thirds of the way through. Oddly enough, the decline seems to set in just after what is probably the best-known poem in the sequence, the 'Floating Poem' (unnumbered, but printed between XIV and XV), has celebrated the lovers' female sexuality:

> Whatever happens between us, your body
> will haunt mine . . .
> . . . your strong tongue and slender fingers
> reaching where I had been waiting years for you
> in my rose-wet cave – whatever happens, this.

The next poem records a failure to transcend circumstances,

asking 'was the failure ours?' (poem XV), and thereafter the relationship seems to go wrong as the poems record more and more dissonance: 'I feel estrangement, yes. As I've felt dawn / pushing towards daybreak' (poem XVIII). The record of progressive estrangement following the declaration of passion 'whatever happens' has an effect similar to Robert Graves's 'Dialogue on a Headland' which opens with a similar declaration:

> SHE: You'll not forget these rocks and what I told you?
> HE: How could I? Never: whatever happens.[62]

The ominous phrase opens up a Pandora's box of mistrust between the lovers which destroys their idyll; similarly with Rich's sequence, which begins ecstatically and ends in solitude. There is an elegiac note discernible in a late poem:

> this we were, this is how we tried to love,
> and these are the forces they had ranged against us
> and these are the forces we had ranged within us,
> within us and against us, against us and within us.
>
> (Poem XVII)

Rich has claimed, as a lesbian separatist, that the new language of poetry has to do with articulation of woman-centred sexuality, and 'Twenty-One Love Poems' should, I think, be construed as attempts at the forging of new forms (although, compared with *The Lesbian Body*, they look positively conventional). Certainly the poems do meditate, with more than a tinge of personal bitterness, on the paradoxes of language encountered by the lovers, notably the distance between experience and its articulation, the difficulty of speech and the need for an honest response, and the problem of getting beyond repeating the same story endlessly:

> You're telling the story of your life
> for once, a tremor breaks the surface of your words.

The story of our lives becomes our lives.

(Poem XVIII)

But I am not clear that these problems, as presented in the poems, are really specific to women. The gap between experience and language is, after all, a philosophical problem that applies to all speakers, whether they know it or not. What defines these love-poems as feminist is their subject matter and Rich's acknowledged public identity as feminist. But injection of new experiential content is not in itself a transformation of poetry; though Rich, I think, would argue that it is. She has said something close to this, talking about 'Twenty-One Love Poems':

> Two friends of mine, both of them artists, wrote to me about reading *Twenty-One Love Poems* with their male lovers, assuring me how 'universal' the poems were. I found myself angered, and when I asked myself why, I realized that it was anger at having my work essentially assimilated and stripped of its meaning, 'integrated' into heterosexual romance. That kind of 'acceptance' of the book seems to me a refusal of its deepest implications. The longing to simplify, to defuse feminism by invoking 'androgyny' or 'humanism', to assimilate lesbian existence by saying that 'relationship is really all the same, love is always difficult' – I see that as a denial, a kind of resistance, as refusal to read and hear what I've actually written, to acknowledge what I am . . . We're not trying to become part of the old order, misnamed 'universal', which has tabooed us; we are transforming the meaning of universality.[63]

It is not surprising that Rich was angry at her friends' response, which does seem an extraordinarily insensitive misreading of the poems. And her political analysis of the exclusion of lesbians from 'universal' heterosexual discourse is admirable. Feminists rightly attach extreme importance to the articulation of one's experience, which can't be thought and therefore in a sense doesn't exist unless it can be named and articulated;[64] and the denial in the form of wilful misunderstanding which Rich relates here certainly impedes the task of articulation. But however important it is to recognize the lesbian experience which these poems meditate on, it does not follow that the language or form of the poetry is specifically female: there is nothing intrinsically gendered about free verse.

A different series of problems in defining a female identity in language is presented by Emily Dickinson. Whereas the writers discussed in this chapter are, with the presumable exception of Irigaray, explicitly lesbian, Dickinson's sex-life is a much-speculated-on mystery. Consequently, more than with Warner's poem and much more than with Rich's, work needs to be separated from the woman, to be read as fantasy rather than with reference to biographical information. Her love-poems, only a handful of which I am discussing here, but which could easily be the subject of a whole book, are famous for their extraordinary directness:

> I gave myself to Him
> And took Himself for pay
>
> (Poem 580)*

But a close examination of such apparently simple declarations elicits, time and again, contradictory meanings of repudiation, or irony, or simply desire rendered impossible by an unreachably distant object:

> The Fruit perverse to plucking
> But leaning to the Sight

---

* Poems are identified by their numbering in *The Complete Poems of Emily Dickinson*, ed. Thomas H. Johnson, 1970.

> With the ecstatic limit
> Of unobtained Delight.
>   (1209)

When Dickinson writes in the delighted or more often
agonized first-person which she deploys in her love-
poems, she is so elusive as to escape final definition: the
poems are riddles with at least two equally convincing
answers. This is apparent in a well-known and comparatively straightforward poem:

> Wild Nights – Wild Nights!
>   Were I with Thee
> Wild Nights should be
>   Our luxury!
>
> Futile the Winds –
>   To a Heart in port –
> Done with the Compass –
>   Done with the Chart!
>
> Rowing in Eden –
>   Ah, the Sea!
> Might I but moor – Tonight
>   In Thee!
>   (249)

This passionate poem articulates desire for a person
whose presence promises dangerous, reckless excess at the
same time as complete protection from disturbance –
interpretations which logically contradict each other.
'Wild Nights should be / Our luxury!' evokes a discharge
of energy sensed as forbidden excess, but it is entirely
ambiguous whether the luxury is the storm of desire or
the promise of shelter from it. Similar contradictions are
at work in the second stanza: you are 'done with the
compass' when you are safe at home, yet the exultancy of
the lines suggests an abandonment so total that the
speaker, lost in mid-ocean, no longer cares to know

where she is. Again, the significance of 'Ah, the Sea!' is uncertain: does the sea represent her lover or divide her from him (or her)? If the storm and the sea represent a tumultuous sexual energy desired by the 'I', they cannot logically also represent threats which she dreams of superseding. (One can, of course, try to resolve these contradictions by saying that the poem dramatizes internal divisions. But that explanation comes close to reading the poems in terms of the poet's hypothetically divided psyche, which is a dubious approach to any poet and particularly inappropriate for Dickinson; and in any case doesn't really explain the problem so much as repeat it.) This teasing uncertainty is a feature of the still more puzzling poem 284:

> The Drop, that wrestles in the Sea –
> Forgets her own locality
> As I – toward Thee –
>
> She knows herself an incense small –
> Yet *small* – she sighs – if *All* – is *All* –
> How larger be?
>
> The Ocean – smiles – at her Conceit –
> But *she*, forgetting Amphitrite –
> Pleads, 'Me?'

This gnomic fable of the Drop, aroused by love to wrestle for her own identity, is structured on a contradiction. The difficult middle stanza seems to be about self-definition: if she concedes that the ocean, being infinite, 'is *All*' – that is, already includes her – how, 'sighs' the Drop, can she add to it? She arrogantly demands that the ocean should be infinitely minus one: herself. This claim seems absurdly arrogant in view of the fact that the sea has swallowed bigger things than her, and (if we are to identify it – or rather him – with the sea-god Poseidon, as I think the classical reference means we must) already has a wife, the sea-nymph Amphitrite.[65] She is an indistinguishable 'drop', identified with dissolving incense that sighs itself out as an adoring breath. Nothing but the will to be herself makes her exist as 'Me', and yet the identity by which she escapes annihilation by the smiling ocean is her selfless love. And though the self-definition and self-surrender which characterize her 'Me?' are both aspects of love, it is difficult to see how they can be so simultaneously. The poem leaves the reader apparently wedged in contradiction. Dickinson's love-poems mostly seem, like Marvell's *Definition of Love*, to be 'begotten by Despair / Upon Impossibility'.

Another, much better-known instance of the contradictoriness of desire as Dickinson articulates it, is poem 640:

> I cannot live with You
> It would be Life –
> And Life is over there –
> Behind the Shelf
>
> The Sexton keeps the Key to –
> Putting up
> Our Life – His Porcelain
> Like a Cup –
>
> Discarded of the Housewife –
> Quaint or Broke –
> A newer Sevres pleases –
> Old Ones crack –
>
> I could not die with You
> For One must wait
> To shut the Other's Gaze down –
> You – could not
>
> And I – Could I stand by
> And see You – freeze –

Without my Right of Frost –
Death's privilege?

Nor could I rise with You
Because your Face
Would put out Jesus' –
That new Grace

Glow plain – and foreign –
On my homesick Eye –
Except that You than He
Stood closer by –

They'd judge us – How –
For you – served Heaven – You know,
Or sought to –
I could not –

Because You saturated Sight –
And I had no more Eyes
For sordid excellence
As Paradise –

And were You lost, I would be
Though My Name
Rang loudest
On the Heavenly fame –

And were You saved –
And I – compelled to be
Where You were not –
That Self – were Hell to me –

So We must meet apart
You there – I here –
With just the Door ajar
That Oceans are – and Prayer –

> And that White Sustenance —
> Despair —

This poem is structured by Christian concepts which the speaker takes as the only imaginable laws of existence, but refuses to live by. The experience begins as secular (being excluded from life which is locked away from the 'Sexton' guardian of death), but the second half traverses the Four Last Things: death, judgment, Hell and Heaven, finding no place in any of them for the desire which constitutes her being. These painful complexities reach their climax in the final stanza, especially its concluding words 'that White Sustenance — Despair —', which is I think to be associated with the white manna renewed daily for the children of Israel on their journey in the wilderness,[66] which symbolizes the promise of salvation and in Christian exegesis is sometimes allegorically interpreted as a symbol of the bread of the Eucharist. In Dickinson's despairing poem, the manna represents not promise but prohibition: the poet arrogantly refuses to pretend to a desire for heaven she does not feel, but only heaven can give her what she does want. There is a sense in which she does feed on the irreducible hope implied in the capacity to go on existing; but, living on separation and 'prayer' — which could only be granted if she abandoned her arrogantly disobedient desire — she can only implore release from the inexorable laws which separate the lovers. It is like a harsher version of the woman's dilemma in Christina Rossetti's 'Monna Innominata'; but whereas the 'Unnamed Lady' repudiates the idea that she might love a man more than God — 'Trust me, I have not earned your dear rebuke'[67] — Dickinson's poem turns on that very claim; as she says, outrageously, she doesn't *need* Him. But equally, she doesn't expect to win: though she rejects the whole apparatus of God, Hell and Heaven, they remain the language of her thought. What is complex in the poem is not her argument with God – this is clear enough: she wants heaven on her own terms of secular desire, which she knows cannot be granted – but the psychological dilemma enacted and resolved, ending with the impossibility which began it. The drama is entirely subjective, comprising both the agonizing separation (the cup locked away from a shelf so that no one can drink from it) and her own incapacity to conform like her lover to Heaven's demands, so that 'I cannot live with You' means both 'I am incapable' and 'I am prevented'. How you read the poem depends on where you draw the line between these interpretations of 'cannot': even in this direct declaration, Dickinson leaves us uncertain of the meaning.

Dickinson's irony and duplicity prevent one from discovering with certainty a representation of specifically female experience in her poems, it being indeterminable exactly what the experience they articulate really is. We are often left in doubt – whether or in what degree a poem is to be taken ironically, as with poem 1072, 'Title Divine – is Mine!', which concludes:

> 'My Husband' – Women say
> Stroking the Melody
> Is *this* – the way?

Is that last line triumph, or is it fastidious distaste? Again, poem 580 follows an unforgettably resonant opening with a suggestion of a bad bargain:

> I gave myself to Him
> And took Himself for pay,
> Yet hesitating Fragments – both
> Surveyed Eternity –
>
> . . . .
>
> But till the Merchant buy
> Still Fable – in the Isles of Spice
> The subtle Cargoes – lie –

> At least — 'tis Mutual Risk —
> Some — found it Mutual Gain —
> Sweet Debt of Life — Each Night to owe —
> Insolvent — every Noon —

This is, needless to say, beautiful as well as erotic. Yet its metaphor of circular exchange, with the payment passing endlessly between the cosy couple, suggests a certain scepticism about actual as opposed to anticipated pleasure; at least, it is assigned to 'some', not to the imagined self.

The gender of the speakers of Dickinson's love-poems is also often something of a riddle. This is obviously true of the two versions of poem 540, 'Going to Him! Happy Letter!' and 'Going to Her! Happy Letter!', where the difference of meaning according to the choice of pronoun is surprisingly great; or, more mysteriously, poem 518 about the disappearing bride:

> Her sweet Weight on my heart a night
> Had scarcely deigned to lie,
> When stirring, for Belief's delight
> My Bride had slipped away.

This is a kind of erotic ghost-story, the gender of whose speaker is indeterminate; s/he certainly doesn't sound at all like a lawful bridegroom. The last line comes as a real shock: 'stirring, for Belief's delight' is so highly charged a phrase that it plainly ought to describe lovemaking. But not so: the awakening which should have confirmed a delight past belief is empty, and the use of the pluperfect ('had slipped away') unobtrusively doubles her distance: even within the telling, she had slipped away into the past. It is left, typically, uncertain whether the experience was real or not:

> If 'twas a Dream — made solid — just
> The Heaven to confirm
> Or if Myself were dreamed of Her
> The power to presume

> With Him remain – who unto me
> Gave – even as to All –
> A Fiction superseding Faith
> By so much – as 'twas real.

The bride's disappearance ought, rationally speaking, to prove her non-existent, but Dickinson makes the speaker insist that she is 'real', whether because the speaker's own dream came true, or because the vanished bride actually dreamt herself into the poet's bed. The mention of God leads one to expect that a miracle will be claimed (the poem, consonantly with its story, keeps promising and withholding satisfaction), but on the contrary, the speaker has been given the privilege only of an experience transcending belief in proportion to its own reality – a 'reality' which is, of course, impossible for the speaker to gauge; only God knows, and He isn't saying. The sceptic could say that what everyone is granted is the capacity to be enthralled by their own delusion. Dickinson evades defining the status of the experience: the poem remains ambiguous.

Dickinson's poems, then, are remarkably difficult to assimilate into a theory of female identity articulating itself through the writing of an Imaginary relationship between an 'I' and a 'Thou', which could constitute a textual 'space' for specifically female meaning. They are too ambiguous and contradictory to be read as purely woman-centred texts. Dickinson uses such a variety of voices and positions to speak from that though she excels in poems which create an identity through reflection and opposition to a beloved, these seem characterized less by transcendence of gender than by irony, evasion and ambiguity. They are unsatisfactory if considered as poetic renderings of an Irigarayan female Imaginary: the only way in which Dickinson obviously conforms to Irigaray's account of female discourse being her indeterminable meanings and her contradictoriness.

6 Conclusion

A close examination of these women-centred love-poems reveals, then, that Irigaray's positing of female identity and language as flowing from an Imaginary source specific to women is (characteristically enough) ambiguous as a means of defining a feminist poetics. Irigaray has made a subtle and convincing analysis of the effacement of women from masculine discourses, especially those of philosophy and psychoanalysis, and of women's alienation in language. Her articulation of specifically female meaning and of women's sexual identity through metaphors of fluidity is immensely suggestive, however difficult her use of these terms can be to follow. The rightness of these metaphors is confirmed by the frequence with which imagery of water, oceans and dissolution is associated in women's poems with identity and sexuality, not only in the work of the poets discussed above (every one of whom makes such an association) but also in the lesbian erotic poetry discussed in Chapter 3 (pp. 74–6). Irigaray's insistence on the need to recognize the existence of specifically female sexuality also makes admirable psychoanalytic sense: in retrospect, it seems extraordinary that she should have been attacked so furiously for arguing that psychoanalysis, as theorized by Freud, Klein and Lacan, has never recognized, let along analysed, the specific pleasures and fantasies associated with the female body: a criticism which is undeniably accurate.

But there are problems with Irigaray's theories of women's identity as a source of definition for feminist poetics, particularly the association of this identity with an Imaginary mode of being, which she articulates beautifully in the mono/duologue 'When our lips speak together', and which informs much of her writing about women's alienation. The difficulty can be put first in psychoanalytic terms. Since the Imaginary realm is defined originally in terms of infantile narcissism, the female Imaginary mode of being must exist in and flow from the relationship between the girl baby and her mother during the period of the baby's absolute dependence, before she negotiates the anxieties of the castration complex. Unlike the Oedipal drama in which she will shortly be cast as an actor, the little girl's Imaginary fantasies do not represent her mother as an object for which her desire must compete with the male, her father: the good/bad breast has no gender. But if sexual difference is irrelevant to the Imaginary mode of being, then the latter cannot be defined as specifically female. This problem emerged very clearly from Wittig's *The Lesbian Body* (see above, pp. 156–8) – a text which, of all those which this chapter looks at, comes closest to constituting a female Imaginary world through disruptive experiments with language. Wittig's very success in writing the anonymous 'j/e' whose words engage with the most primitive energies and structures of Imaginary fantasy, in which identity depends on the presence of the loved one, not on sexual difference, makes the text's fantasy slide out of its otherwise women-centred world of meaning.

An equal difficulty arises from the attempt to theorize a female Imaginary identity from women's writing: the problem of the language by which it is to be created, or at least glimpsed. (This is actually the same problem as the first, but seen from a reverse angle.) The Imaginary mode of being is archaic, dating from a time before the castration complex, and before language was acquired – the dual event which begins the history of human subject. In the psychoanalytic thought from which the concept of the Imaginary is drawn, the entry into the system of significant differences which is language coincides with the conception of sexual difference organized around the presence or absence of the phallus, or privileged signifier. This coincidence of signifying activity with sexual difference means that the project of writing a female Imaginary identity is utopian in the negative sense of being unrealistic. The traces of the opposite sex can never be entirely effaced from a woman's text: a difficulty which emerged in a very simple and literal way from the Warner and Dickinson poems discussed above – that is the way that a masculine persona, or even a small masculine pronoun, disrupts what could otherwise be thought of as purely female discourse.

It is true that these problems could disappear if feminists accepted the separatist, lesbian feminist analysis which underpins the poetry of Adrienne Rich, and which locates female identity in 'that *primary presence of women to each other* . . . which is the crucible of a new language'.[68] This analysis has points in common with Irigaray's: notably, the insistence on the need to understand female sexuality in its own terms, on the importance of the little girl's earliest bond with her mother, and on the possibility of developing a language to articulate the identity emerging from love between women – Rich's 'whole new poetry beginning here'.[69] The arguments for such a notion of pure female identity are coherent; the trouble with them is that they oversimplify the issues drastically, depending on a female nature (good) corrupted by patriarchal culture (bad) to submit itself to 'compulsory heterosexuality'.[70] The poetry of woman-centred sexuality which emerged from this analysis is not, as it has been claimed to be,[71] a new language because it articulates women's authentic experience: because experience and language do not coincide, and there is nothing gendered about poetic form.

A poetry of purely female identity is not, then, a really viable possibility, whether it is imagined in the language of radical feminism or in Irigaray's post-Lacanian terms. Apart from the utopian 'When Our Lips Speak Together', the examples of women's poetry which ought to correspond to Imaginary femaleness always turn out, when looked at closely, to be engaged with the same masculine language or symbolism which they are supposed to transcend. But this oppositional engagement, this struggle to transform inherited meanings, is where the real strength and specifity of women's poetry lies. Certainly, it is true that the notion of specifically female language and identity is utopian, like that of a female tradition of poetry written without reference to any masculine discourse. But the value of utopias is that they enable us to imagine possibilities of difference for the brute, contingent world 'which is the world / Of all of us, the place where, in the end, / We find our happiness, or not at all'.[72] It is a world which is dominated by class and race oppression, and by masculine privilege which does not only exert its power at the level of representation. The refusal to concede these privileges is implied in the creation of an alternative realm of female identity; like all the poetry examined in this book, it both comes out of and helps to make possible women's struggle to transform the meanings of our world.

NOTES

1 INTRODUCTORY

1 For discussion of the critical and scholarly neglect of women poets, see essays by Adrienne Rich, especially those on Anne Bradstreet and Eleanor Ross Taylor, collected in *On Lies, Secrets and Silence* (1980, hereafter referred to as *OLSS*); also Tillie Olsen's *Silences* (1979).

2 See, for example, John Cody, *After Great Pain: The Inner Life of Emily Dickinson* (Belknap Press of Harvard University Press, 1971); and Richard Howard, 'Sylvia Plath: "And I Have No Face, I Have Wanted to Efface Myself" ', in *The Art of Sylvia Plath: A Symposium*, ed. Charles Newman (Indiana University Press, Bloomington, 1970) pp. 77–88.

3 For published accusations of female inadequacy, see Theodore Roethke's objections to women poets, quoted by S. Gilbert and S. Gubar, *The Madwoman in the Attic* (1979) p. 541. On the same page they quote from James Reeves's introduction to his selection from Dickinson's poems: 'A friend who is a literary critic has suggested, not perhaps quite seriously, that a woman poet is a contradiction in terms.' See also the section 'Phallic Criticism' in Mary Ellmann's *Thinking About Woman* (1979), especially pp. 33–7, on the critical reception of Plath's poems.

4 Anne Bradstreet, 'The Prologue', stanza 5. Collected in *Salt and Bitter and Good*, ed. Cora Kaplan (1975).

5 But see Judy Grahn, *Another Mother Tongue* (1984)

6 An early statement by Adrienne Rich is relevant here: 'instead of poems *about* experience I am getting poems that are experiences' (*Poetry and Experience*, 1964: see *Adrienne Rich's Poetry*, ed. Barbara and Albert Gelpi, 1975, p. 90).

7 This emphasis on the authenticity of women's experience as the key to women's poetry is apparent in all Rich's essays (including that cited in n. 6 above) and in Suzanne Juhasz's *Naked and Fiery Forms* (1976).

8   See especially the essays by Sandra Gilbert on Sylvia Plath, Jane Stanborough on Edna St Vincent Millay, and Suzanne Juhasz on Anne Sexton in *Shakespeare's Sisters*, ed. Gilbert and Gubar, (1979).

9   See Rich's essays on Eleanor Ross Taylor and Judy Grahn in *OLSS*, and her quotations from H.D. prefacing *The Dream of a Common Language* (1978).

10 'The Intentional Fallacy' by W.K. Wimsatt and Monroe Beardsley, collected in W.K. Wimsatt, *The Verbal Icon* (1954).

11 Rich's poem 'Frame' is collected in *A Wild Patience Has Taken Me This Far* (1981), and Judy Grahn's 'A Woman Is Talking to Death' is collected in *The Work of a Common Woman* (1978).

12 R. Graves, 'To Juan at the Winter Solstice', in *Poems Selected by Himself* (1974). For a critique of explanations of texts in terms of authorial personality, see the writings of Roland Barthes, especially 'The Death of the Author' in *Image – Music – Text*, (ed. and trans. Stephen Heath, 1979), and *The Pleasure of the Text* (1975).

13 Boris Pasternak, *I Remember* (New York, Pantheon, 1962), p. 62. Quoted by Denise Levertov in 'Notebook Pages', *The Poet in the World* (New Directions, New York, 1973), p. 16.

14 Quoted from section 11 of 'Tribute to the Angels' in *Trilogy* by H.D. (1973.)

15 From Lilian Mohin's introduction to *One Foot on the Mountain* (1979), pp. 1–2.

16 From Rich's essay 'Power and Danger: The Works of a Common Woman', *OLSS*, p. 248.

17 See Lilian Mohin's collection *Cracks* (Onlywomen, 1978), and her poems in *One Foot on the Mountain* including 'This dream recurs (and is not obscure)'.

18 See Mary Gentile's article 'Adrienne Rich and Separatism: The Language of Multiple Realities', *Maenad*, vol. 2, no. 2 (Winter 1982), and, more obliquely, Susan Friedman, 'I go where I love: an intertextual study of H.D. and Adrienne Rich', *Signs*, vol. 9, no. 2 (Winter 1984).

19 See Randall Jarrell's essays 'A Note on Poetry' and 'The End of the Line', collected in *Kipling, Auden & Co.* (1981).

20 William Wordsworth, Preface to *Lyrical Ballads* (1805), ed. D. Roper (1964), p. 35.

21 *Ibid.*, p. 37.

22 *Ibid.*, p. 42.

23 *Ibid.*, p. 29.

24 Francis Jeffrey, review of Southey in *Edinburgh Review*, vol. 1, no. 1 (1802); extract reprinted in D. Roper's edition of *Lyrical Ballads* cited here, pp. 410 and 412.

25 Wordsworth, *op. cit*, pp. 30–1.
26 Sheila Shulman, 'Hard Words, or why lesbians have to be philosophers', printed in *One Foot on the Mountain*, ed. Mohin (1979); quoted from part V of the poem.
27 Wordsworth, *The Prelude*, Book IV ('Summer Vacation'), l. 332.
28 Rich, 'Power and Danger', *OLSS*, p. 248.
29 L. Mohin, introduction to *One Foot on the Mountain*, p. 4; and see n. 15 above.
30 Mary Gentile, *op. cit.*, p. 142 (see n. 18 above).
31 See Carmen Williams, 'White Woman, Hey', printed in *Feminist Review*, no. 17 (Autumn 1984), p. 79. See also the article 'Challenging Imperial Feminism' by Valerie Amos and Pratibha Parmar in the same issue.
32 From the preface by Elly Bulkin and Joan Larkin to *Lesbian Poetry* (1981), p. xi.
33 See Mary Gentile, *op. cit.*, p. 142, on the need for 'evoking the bodily and emotional experiences of *all* women' (my emphasis). For feminist criticism underplaying class differences, see Sandra Gilbert's article surveying women's poetry and prose during the First World War, 'Soldier's Heart: Literary Men, Literary Women, and the Great War', *Signs*, vol. 8, no. 3 (Spring 1983), pp. 422–50. Gilbert reads this work for its proto-feminist anger and exhilaration, stressing female unity but neglecting evidence of inter-class antagonism. For instance she quotes from Nina MacDonald's 'Sing a Song of War-Time' the lines 'Girls are doing things / They've never done before, / Go as 'bus conductors, / Drive a car or van, / All the world is topsy-turvey / Since the war began' (Gilbert, p. 425), omitting the preceding 'Mummie does the house-work, / Can't get any maid, / Gone to make munitions, / 'Cos they're better paid' (see *Scars Upon My Heart*, ed. C. Reilly, 1981, p. 69).
34 Irena Klepfisz, 'Work Sonnets' collected in *Keeper of Accounts* (1982).
35 For feminist critiques of demeaning and distorting images of women in English poetry, see Elizabeth Hampstein's essay 'A Woman's Map of Lyric Poetry', *College English* (May 1973), also Cora Kaplan's introduction to *Salt and Bitter and Good* (1975) and essay 'Language and Gender' (*Papers on Patriarchy*, 1976). See also Germaine Greer, *The Female Eunuch* (1970).
36 Thomas Nash, 'Adieu, farewell earth's bliss'.
37 Cora Kaplan, introduction to *Salt and Bitter and Good*, p. 21.
38 From Lucy Boston, 'Hybrid Perpetual', in *Time is Undone* (1977).
39 *Ibid*.
40 See Ronsard, 'Mignonne, allons voir si la rose'; Spenser, 'Gather

the rose of love while yet is time', Waller's 'Song to the Rose' and Blake's 'Sick Rose'.

41 Sylvia Plath, 'Poppies in July', *Collected Poems*, ed. Ted Hughes (1981).

42 Charlotte Mew, 'The Quiet House', collected in *Salt and Bitter and Good*, ed. Kaplan.

43 Plath, 'Poppies in July'.

44 Shakespeare, *Othello*, Act III, scene iii. For a discussion of the literary associations of poppies see the section 'Roses and Poppies' in ch. VII, 'Arcadian Recourses', of Paul Fussell's *The Great War and Modern Memory* (1975).

45 From 'Girl's gifts' by Alison Fell, collected in *One Foot on the Mountain*, ed. Mohin.

46 Katherine Mansfield, 'Prelude' (1919; printed in *Collected Stories*, 1981).

47 See Horace, *Odes*, Book III, no. xxx, line 1 – 'Exegi monumentum aere perennius' – 'I have completed a work more enduring than bronze'. Cf. also 'Not marble nor the gilded monuments / Of princes, shall outlive this powerful rhyme', Shakespeare's *Sonnets*, LV.

48 Rich, 'Transcendental Etude', *Dream of a Common Language*.

49 These are, in order of publication: Julian Symons, *The Thirties: A Dream Revolved* (1966; rev. edn, 1975); Hugh D. Ford, *A Poets' War: English Poets and the Spanish Civil War* (1965), D.E.S. Maxwell, *Poets of the Thirties* (1969), A.J. Tolley, *Poetry of the 1930s* (1975), Alick West, *Crisis and Criticism and Other Literary Essays* (1975), Samuel Hynes, *The Auden Generation* (1976), Bernard Bergonzi, *Reading the Thirties* (1978), John Lucas (ed.), *The 1930s, a Challenge to Orthodoxy* (1978), Francis Barker *et al.* (eds), *Practices of Literature and Politics* and *The Politics of Modernism* (1979: published proceedings of the Conference on the Sociology of Literature for 1936); Richard Johnstone, *The Will to Believe: Novelists of the Nineteen Thirties* (1982). Martin Green's *Children of the Sun* (1975) covers some of the same ground, with an exclusively androcentric focus.

50 Claud Cockburn, *I, Claud* (1964), p. 187.

51 Richard Crossman (ed.), *The God That Failed* (1950).

52 Skelton, *Poetry of the Thirties* (1964), pp. 28–30.

53 Symons, *The Thirties* (1975), p. 127, for mention of Sitwell and p. 114 for STW.

54 In *The Auden Generation*, Hynes cites Elizabeth Bowen on p. 336, Rosamond Lehmann on pp. 235–7, Naomi Mitchison on p. 116, Storm Jameson on pp. 270–3, and Virginia Woolf on pp. 85 and 392–3.

55 In *Reading the Thirties*, Bergonzi cites Vicki Baum on p. 76, Agatha Christie on pp. 76–7, and Barbara Lucas on p. 129. Garbo is mentioned on pp. 127–33

56 In his memoir of *Left Review* and *Our Time* writers, 'Total Attainder and the Helots' (collected in *The 1930s: A Challenge to Orthodoxy* – see n. 49 above), Arnold Rattenbury does mention Sylvia Townsend Warner (see pp. 139, 140, 144, 152 and 189).

57 See A.J. Tolley's discussion and assessment of the work of Kathleen Raine on pp. 285–8 of *Poetry of the 1930s*.

58 For an admirably detailed and informed discussion of public school influence on writing in the thirties, see the chapter 'Men Among Boys, Boys Among Men', in Bergonzi, *op. cit.*

59 Spender, *World within World* (1953), p. 211.

60 Symons, *op. cit.*, p. 114 (see n. 53 above).

61 For devouring mothers, see Joan Nower in Auden's *Paid on Both Sides* and Mrs Ransom in *The Ascent of F6* by Auden and Isherwood. Mildred Luce in *The Dog Beneath the Skin* (also by Auden and Isherwood) wants to revenge the death of her own son in the Great War on the entire present generation of young men. The Judge's wife in Spender's *Trial of a Judge* likewise welcomes fascism and war as a surrogate revenge for her own barrenness. Isherwood's novels also contain alarming mother-figures: for example, Mrs Lindsay in *All the Conspirators* and Lily Vernon in *The Memorial*. For female sexpots, see Sally Bowles in *Goodbye to Berlin*; more ambiguously, Lou Vipond in *The Dog Beneath the Skin*; and the unnamed temptress in Upward's *Journey to the Border* (1938).

2 WOMEN AND TRADITION

1 Charles Dickens, *Bleak House*, Ch. XIV ('Deportment').

2 Adrienne Rich, 'When We Dead Awaken', *On Lies Secrets and Silence*, p. 39.

3 Adrienne Rich, part 6 of 'Snapshots of a Daughter-in-Law', *Poems Selected and New, 1950–1974* (1975), p. 49.

4 Thomas Campion, 'When to her lute Corinna sings', *A Book of Airs*, vi.

5 Sandra Gilbert and Susan Gubar, *The Madwoman in the Attic*, pp. 38–9.

6 Mary Jacobus, review of *The Madwoman in the Attic* in *Signs*, vol. 6, no. 3 (Spring 1981), p. 517.

7 Gilbert and Gubar, *The Madwoman in the Attic*, p. 113

8 *Ibid.*, p. 71.

9 Matthew Arnold's phrase for Charlotte Brontë's novel *Villette*, quoted in *The Madwoman in the Attic*, p. 337.

10 *The Madwoman in the Attic*, p. 68.
11 *Ibid.*
12 *Ibid.*
13 See the sonnet sequences by Edna St Vincent Millay and Christina Rossetti discussed in Chapter 4; also Elizabeth Barrett Browning's *Sonnets from the Portuguese*; also the sonnets by Louise Labé discussed by Ann Rosalind Jones in 'Assimilation With a Difference: Renaissance Women Poets and Literary Influence', *Yale French Studies* 62 (1981), *Feminist Readings: French Texts/American Contexts*.
14 For a fascinating discussion of the relation between Christina Rossetti and her brother's paintings, see Dolores Rosenblum's essay 'Christina Rossetti: The Inward Pose', collected in *Shakespeare's Sisters*, ed. Gilbert and Gubar (1979).
15 See Tillie Olsen, *Silences* (1979), pp. 127–33, on Hopkins, and *The Madwoman in the Attic*, pp. 3–11, also on Hopkins.
16 For a particularly successful example of a feminist writing collective, see the group of women who produced *Tales I Tell My Mother* (1978): Zoe Fairbairns, Sara Maitland, Michele Roberts, Valerie Miner, Michelene Wandor – all of whom have produced distinguished work.
17 Sylvia Plath, 'The Colossus', *Collected Poems* (1981).
18 Elizabeth Hardwick on Plath, quoted by Tillie Olsen in *Silences*, p. 250.
19 See Joyce Carol Oates, 'Is There a Female Voice?', *Gender and Literary Voice*, ed. Janet Todd (1981).
20 Anne Stevenson, 'Writing as a Woman', collected in *Women Writing and Writing about Women*, ed. Mary Jacobus (1979), pp. 174–5.
21 Anne Stevenson, 'The Poetry of Carol Rumens', *PN Review*, no. 46 (vol. 12, no. 2), p. 50.
22 Anne Stevenson, *ibid.*
23 Anne Stevenson, *Correspondences* (1974), p. 13.
24 *Ibid.*, p. 41.
25 *Ibid.*, p. 34.
26 Anne Stevenson, 'Black Mountain, Green Mountain', *Minute by Glass Minute* (1982).
27 *Ibid.*
28 *Ibid.*
29 See the poems by Caroline Griffin, Alison Fell, Harriet Rose and Diana Scott in *One Foot on the Mountain*, ed. Mohin.
30 Monique Wittig, *The Lesbian Body* (1976), pp. 21 and 32.
31 See Luce Irigaray, 'L'*Hystéra* de Platon', *Speculum de l'autre femme* (1974).

32   For reworking of fairytales, see particularly Angela Carter's *The Bloody Chamber* (1981). Alice Thomas Ellis uses myth as plot-material and source of irony: *The 27th Kingdom* (1981) is loosely based on Lives of the Saints, and *The Other Side of the Fire* (1983) overtly bases its sardonic comedy of romantic illusion on the tragedy of Phaedra. Sara Maitland recasts Greek myths in *Telling Tales* (1984) and Bible stories in *Daughter of Jerusalem* (1980); Michele Roberts's *The Wild Girl* (1984) recasts New Testament material. Other women novelists have used literary classics as myths to be reworked; the classic instance is Jean Rhys with *Jane Eyre* in *The Wide Sargasso Sea* (1966). Emma Tennant in *The Bad Sister* (1969) similarly uses Hogg's *Confessions of a Justified Sinner* as its reference-point.

33   See Rachell Blau Duplessis, 'The Critique of Consciousness and Myth in Levertov, Rich and Rukeyser' in *Shakespeare's Sisters*, ed. Gilbert and Gubar, and Alicia Ostriker, 'The Thieves of Language: Woman Poets and Revisionist Mythmaking', *Signs*, vol. 8, no. 1 (Spring 1982).

34   Alicia Ostriker, 'The Thieves of Language', p. 72.

35   Liddell and Scott, *A Greek–English Lexicon*, concise edition 1901, p. 454.

36   Walter Benjamin, 'The Storyteller: Reflections on the Work of Nikolai Leskov', *Illuminations* (1973), p. 86.

37   *Ibid.*, p. 84.

38   *Ibid.*, p. 89.

39   *Ibid.*, p. 90.

40   *Ibid.*, p. 91.

41   *Ibid.*

42   *Ibid.*, p. 85.

43   Liz Lochhead, 'The Storyteller', *The Grimm Sisters* (1981).

44   Benjamin, 'The Storyteller', *Illuminations*, p. 102.

45   Hermione Lee uses this phrase from Stevie Smith's *Novel on Yellow Paper* to characterize the writer's style in her introduction to Stevie Smith's *Selected Writings* (1983), p. 23.

46   Hermione Lee, *ibid.*, pp. 23–4.

47   Seamus Heaney, *Preoccupations, Selected Prose 1968–1978* (1980), p. 200.

48   W.H. Auden's definition of light verse occurs in the preface to the *Oxford Book of Light Verse* (1938); Benjamin's essay on Leskov first appeared in *Orient and Occident* (1936) (see editor's note to *Illuminations*, p. 268).

49   Stevie Smith, 'The Frog Prince', *Collected Poems* (1975).

50   Stevie Smith, 'I rode with my darling . . .', *Collected Poems*.

51   'Angel Boley' first appeared in the New Statesman on 20

December 1968. It is in *Collected Poems*.
52 See E.M. Wakefield, *The Observer's Book of Fungi* (Frederick Warne, London, 1958), p. 28.
53 Suzanne Juhasz, *Naked and Fiery Forms* (1976), p. 128.
54 Anne Sexton, 'Prologue', *Transformations* (1972).
55 Anne Sexton, 'Snow White', *Transformations*.
56 Bruno Bettelheim, *The Uses of Enchantment* (1978), pp. 210 and 290.
57 Anne Sexton, 'Briar Rose', *Transformations*.
58 Anne Sexton, 'Rapunzel', *ibid*.
59 Olga Broumas, 'Rapunzel', *Beginning with O* (1977).
60 Alicia Ostriker, 'The Thieves of Language', p. 86.
61 T.S. Eliot, 'Tradition and the Individual Talent', *Selected Essays* (1966), p. 16.
62 Liz Lochhead, 'Tam Lin's Lady', *The Grimm Sisters*.
63 *Ibid*.
64 Alicia Ostriker, 'The Thieves of Language', p. 71.

3 TOWARDS A WOMAN'S TRADITION
1 Adrienne Rich, 'When We Dead Awaken: Writing as Re-vision', *On Lies, Secrets and Silence* (1980).
2 *Ibid*., p. 39
3 *Ibid*.
4 *Ibid*., pp. 44–8.
5 See Susan Friedman's article 'I go where I love: An intertextual study of H.D. and Adrienne Rich', *Signs*, vol. 9, no. 2 (1985), which argues this point at length, laying stress on Rich's relation to her 'foremothers'.
6 See Ellen Moers, *Literary Women* (1978), chs 8, 'Loving Heroinism: Feminists in Love', and 15, 'Female Gothic'.
7 Wordsworth, 'A slumber did my spirit seal', *Lyrical Ballads* (1805).
8 Margaret Homans, *Women Writers and Poetic Identity* (1980), p. 216.
9 Title of concluding chapter of *ibid*.
10 For a fully articulated critique of feminist 'essentialism', see Monique Plaza, 'Phallomorphic Power and the Psychology of "woman" ', *Ideology and Consciousness*, no. 4 (Autumn 1978). Although Plaza's attack on Irigaray in this article is misdirected and unfair, her critique of essentialism as a problem in feminist thinking is very useful.
11 Adrienne Rich, 'Power and Danger: The Work of a Common Woman', *OLSS*, p. 250.

12 A.S. Byatt, interviewed in *Women Writers Talking*, ed. Janet Todd (1983), p. 181–95.

13 'Of Holy Writing and Priestly Voices: A Talk with Esther Broner', *Massachusetts Review*, vol. xxi, no. 2 (Summer 1983), p. 259.

14 Adrienne Rich, 'For Julia in Nebraska', *A Wild Patience Has Taken Me This Far* (1981).

15 Peter Levi, 'Christmas Sermon', *Collected Poems* (1975).

16 Willa Cather's novels were out of print in the UK until reissued by Virago Press.

17 Malcolm Bradbury, in *The Modern American Novel* (1983), does not discuss Willa Cather's work.

18 I must stress that these remarks do not apply to Catherine Reilly's second anthology of women's war poetry, *Chaos of the Night* (Virago, 1984), a collection of women poets of World War II.

19 Vera Brittain, 'To My Brother', *Scars Upon My Heart*, ed. Catherine Reilly (1981).

20 See *Scars Upon My Heart*, ed. Reilly, p. 15n.

21 Paul Fussell, *The Great War and Modern Memory* (1975), chs V, 'Oh What A Literary War' and VII, 'Arcadian Recourses'.

22 To give some of these literary and nature references in detail: Margaret Cole's 'The Falling Leaves' alludes to a well-known simile in Milton's *Paradise Lost* (compare 'a gallant multitude / Which now all withering lay ... Like snowflakes falling on the Flemish clay' with the fallen angels lying 'thick as autumnal leaves that strow the brooks', a simile also cited by Fussell, *op cit.*, p. 166; S. Gertrude Ford's 'Armistice Day' recalls 'Lycidas': compare Milton's 'Bid Amaranthus all his beauty shed' with 'Let the red rose of England burn away / And Amaranth, for the life that never dies'. Catherine Whetham's 'The Poet and the Butcher' is an (unsuccessful) parody of the 'organ voices' of Milton and Wordsworth: Aelfrida Tillyard's 'Invitation au Festin' brings off its allusions to Marlowe's 'Come live with me and be my love' more wittily. More obliquely, Lilian Anderson's narrative of the airman's journey over England in 'Leave in 1917' clearly engages with the traditions of Romantic and Victorian landscape verse – the presences of Keats, Arnold and Hardy are all discernible – while Elizabeth Daryush's 'Flanders Fields' clearly gets its tone and cadence ('Here, where sorrow still must tread / All her graves are garlanded') as well as its stanza form from Shelley's 'Music, when soft voices die'. For more poems mentioning flowers, see also Maud Anna Bell's 'From a Trench', Vera Brittain's 'Perhaps', Charlotte Mew's 'June 1915', Alice Meynell's 'Summer in England, 1914', Edith Nesbit's 'The Fields of Flanders' and

'Spring in Wartime', Eileen Newton's 'Revision' and Aimee Byng Scott's 'July 1st 1916'. All these poems are printed in *Scars Upon My Heart*, ed. Reilly.

23 Eleanor Farjeon, 'Easter Monday: in memoriam E.T.', *Scars Upon My Heart*, ed. Reilly.

24 Enid Bagnold, *A Diary Without Dates* (1919: reprinted 1978), p. 90.

25 See Sandra Gilbert, 'Costumes of the Mind: Transvestism as Metaphor in Modern Literature', in *Writing and Sexual Difference*, ed. Elizabeth Abel (1982), and 'Soldier's Heart: Literary Men, Literary Women, and the Great War', *Signs*, vol. 8, no. 3 (Spring 1983).

26 Sandra Gilbert, 'Soldier's Heart', *Signs*, vol. 8, no. 3, p. 425.

27 The phrase 'the old sow that eats her farrow' is taken from Stephen Dedalus on Ireland (James Joyce, *A Portrait of the Artist as a Young Man*, 1916, p. 208); but a similar evocation of murderous maternity is discernible in Robert Graves's reprinting of the notorious letter to the Editor of the *Morning Post* from 'A Little Mother', extolling the sacrifices of sons, in *Goodbye to All That* (1929), pp. 202–4.

28 Elly Bulkin and Joan Larkin (eds), *Lesbian Poetry: An Anthology* (1981); introduction, 'A Look at Lesbian Poetry', p. xxiv.

29 *Ibid.*, p. xxvi.

30 *Ibid.*, p. xxiii.

31 Adrienne Rich, *Compulsory Heterosexuality and Lesbian Existence* (Onlywomen, 1981), pp. 20–1.

32 Sheila Shulman, 'Hard Words, or Why Lesbians Have to Be Philosophers', *One Foot on the Mountain*, ed. Mohin.

33 Judy Grahn, 'A Woman Is Talking to Death', part 2, *The Work of a Common Woman* (1978).

34 Audre Lorde, 'Power', *The Black Unicorn* (1978)

35 Judy Grahn, 'A Woman Is Talking to Death', part 1, *The Work of a Common Woman*.

36 Adrienne Rich, 'Transcendental Etude', *The Dream of a Common Language* (1978).

37 Joan Larkin, 'Some Unsaid Things', *Housework* (1982).

38 Olga Broumas, 'Amazon Twins', *Beginning with O* (1977).

39 Olga Broumas, 'Artemis', *Beginning with O*.

40 Judy Grahn, 'She Who Continues', *The Work of a Common Woman*.

41 William Blake, 'Proverbs of Hell'.

42 Adrienne Rich, 'Power and Danger: the work of a common woman', *On Lies, Secrets and Silence*, p. 248.

43 See Robert Graves, *The White Goddess* (1948); and Robert Bly,

Sleepers Joining Hands (1973), especially its central prose section 'I Came Out of the Mother Naked', pp. 29–50.

44 Adrienne Rich, 'The Spirit of Place', part v, *A Wild Patience Has Taken Me This Far* (1981).

45 Audre Lorde, '125th Street and Abomey', *The Black Unicorn.* Seboulisa is glossed in an explanatory note as 'the mother of us all' (see *The Black Unicorn*, p. 121).

46 Audre Lorde, note on Yemanja, *ibid.*, pp. 121–2.

47 Audre Lorde, 'From the house of Yemanja', *ibid.*

48 Audre Lorde, 'Coniagui Women', *ibid.*

49 Audre Lorde, 'The Same Death Over and Over, or, Lullabies Are for Children', *ibid.*

50 Adrienne Rich, 'Power and Danger', *OLSS*, p. 248.

51 Judy Grahn, foreword to 'A Woman Is Talking to Death', *The Work of a Common Woman*, p. 112.

52 Judy Grahn, 'She Who / She Who carries herself', *ibid.*

53 Judy Grahn, 'A funeral', *ibid.*

54 Judy Grahn, 'Carol and', *ibid.*

55 Judy Grahn, 'The most blonde woman', *ibid.*

56 Judy Grahn 'I am the wall', *ibid.*

57 Rosalind Coward, *Patriarchal Precedents* (1983), chapter 2, 'The Meaning of Mother-right'.

58 Dorothy Dinnerstein, *The Mermaid and the Minotaur* (1977), p. 203.

59 Adrienne Rich, 'Natural Resources', part 4, *The Dream of a Common Language.*

60 Adrienne Rich, 'Diving into the Wreck', *Poems Selected and New* (1975).

61 *Ibid.*

62 Adrienne Rich, 'To a Poet', *The Dream of a Common Language.*

63 See the poems 'Power', 'Phantasia for Elvira Shatayev' and 'Paula Becker to Clara Westhoff', Adrienne Rich, *The Dream of A Common Language.*

64 Adrienne Rich, 'From an Old House in America', abridged from parts 2 and 3; see *Poems Selected and New.*

65 Adrienne Rich, 'Natural Resources', part 11, *The Dream of a Common Language.*

66 *Ibid.*

67 H.D., 'The Walls Do Not Fall', part 1, *Trilogy* (1973).

68 Adrienne Rich, 'Culture and Anarchy', *A Wild Patience Has Taken Me This Far.*

69 Adrienne Rich, 'Transcendental Etude', *The Dream of a Common Language.*

70 Adrienne Rich, 'Turning the Wheel', part 6, 'Apparition', *A Wild*

Patience Has Taken Me This Far.
71   Adrienne Rich, 'Turning the Wheel', part 5, 'Particularity'.
72   *Ibid.*, part 2, 'Burden Baskets'.
73   Irena Klepfisz, *'Bashert'*, part 2 ('Chicago 1964': 'I am walking home alone at midnight'), *Keeper of Accounts* (1982).
74   *Ibid.*
75   *Ibid.*
76   *Ibid.*
77   Carol Rumens, 'Outside Oswiecim', stanza 10. Poem collected in *Time Present and Time Past*, ed. Marion Lomax (1985).
78   Carol Rumens, 'Outside Oswiecim', stanza 13.
79   Irena Klepfisz, *'Bashert'*, part 4, *Keeper of Accounts*.

4 TWO-WAY MIRRORS
1   Jan Montefiore, 'The Mistress to her Lover', collected in *Time Present and Time Past*, ed. Marion Lomax (1985), p. 23.
2   See Frederick Goldin, *The Mirror of Narcissus* (1964), pp. 1–15.
3   Gilbert and Gubar, *The Madwoman in the Attic*, p. 68.
4   Quoted from Gayatri Chakravorty Spivak, 'French Feminism in an International Frame', *Yale French Studies*, no. 62 (1981): *Feminist Readings: French Texts, American Contexts*, p. 171, paraphrasing the entry under 'Imaginary' in J. Laplanche and J.P. Pontalis, *The Language of Psychoanalysis* (1973), p. 210.
5   Jacques Lacan, 'The Mirror Stage as Formative of the Function of the I', *Ecrits* (1977), p. 2.
6   *Ibid.*, pp. 1–2.
7   *Ibid.*, p. 2.
8   'But the important point is that this form situated the agency of the ego, before its social determination, in a fictional direction, which will always remain irreducible for the individual alone, or rather, which will only rejoin the coming-into-being (*le devenir*) of the object asymptomatically' (*ibid.*).
9   See section 5 of the entry 'Absence' in Roland Barthes's *A Lover's Discourse* (1978), p. 15, quoted below (p. 106); also n. 28 of this chapter, below.
10   Freud, *Beyond the Pleasure Principle* (1974), p. 9n.
11   Maud Mannoni, *The Child, his 'Illness' and the Others* (1973), p. 16.
12   Jacqueline Rose, in Jacqueline Rose and Juliet Mitchell, *Feminine Sexuality* (1983), p. 30.
13   D.W. Winnicott, *Playing and Reality* (1980), chapter 9, 'The Mirror-Role of Mother and Family in Child Development', p. 138.
14   Nancy Chodorow, *The Reproduction of Mothering* (1978), p. 67.

15   Juliet Mitchell, in Rose and Mitchell, *Feminine Sexuality*, p. 16.

16   See Elizabeth Wilson's article 'Psychoanalysis: Psychic Law and Order', *Feminist Review*, no. 8 (Summer 1981), and Janet Sayers 'Psychoanalytic and Personal Politics: A Response to Elizabeth Wilson', *Feminist Review*, no. 10 (Spring 1982).

17   See Juliet Mitchell, *Psychoanalysis and Feminism* (1976).

18   T.H. White, journal entry quoted by Sylvia Townsend Warner in *T.H. White: A Biography* (1967), p. 288.

19   See S.T. Warner, *op. cit.*, especially ch. XII, 'Alderney 1957–60'.

20   Roland Barthes, *Fragments d'un discours amoureux* (1977), p. 21 (my translation).

21   Lacan, 'Direction de la cure', quoted by Maud Mannoni in *The Child, His 'Illness' and the Others*, p. 60n.

22   See Melanie Klein's account of 'Dick' in the essay 'Symbol-Formation in the Development of the Ego', *Love, Guilt and Reparation* (1975), and the case-history of 'Leon' in Maud Mannoni, *op. cit.*, pp. 85–90, and 213–17.

23   Maud Mannoni, *op. cit.*, p. 19

24   An exception to this rule is Ann Rosalind Jones's fine study of Renaissance women sonneteers, 'Assimilation with a Difference: Renaissance Women Poets and Literary Influence', in Yale French Studies, no. 62 (1981) *Feminist Readings: French Texts/American Contexts*.

25   See Roland Barthes, *S/Z* (1975), Pierre Macherey, *A Theory of Literary Production* (1978), and Julia Kristeva, *Semiotike: Recherches pour une semanalyse* (Tel Quel, Paris, 1969).

26   See, for example, W.H. Auden's introduction to Shakespeare's *Sonnets* (Signet edition, 1964), suggesting that they represent a desperate attempt by the poet to preserve the integrity of a vision which his lover 'seemed intent on covering with mud' (introduction to Shakespeare's *Sonnets*, Signet, 1964, p. xxxiii). This comment sounds as if it originates in Auden's own troubled relationship with the notoriously unfaithful Chester Kallmann.

27   S. Freud, 'A Case of Female Homosexuality', *Penguin Freud*, vol. 9 (*Case Histories*, ii) (1979), p. 380.

28   Roland Barthes, *Fragments d'un discours amoureux* (my translation); 'Absence', p. 20.

29   Frederick Goldin, *op. cit.*, p. 103.

30   *Ibid.*, p. 4.

31   *Ibid.*, p. 14.

32   *Ibid.*, p. 78.

33   *Ibid.*, p. 78.

34   *Ibid.*, p. 92.

35   *Ibid.*, p. 99.

36 *Ibid.*, p. 67.

37 *Ibid.*, pp. 98–9.

38 The coincidence arises partly because Irigaray and Goldin are analysing some of the same material; for example, Goldin cites the following quotation from Plotinus: 'As in a mirror the semblance is in one place, the substance in another so that Matter seems to be full when it is empty, and contains nothing while seeming to contain all things. The copies and shadows which pass in and out of it, come into it as formless shadow. They are seen in it because it has no form of its own' (*ibid.*, p. 6). Irigaray quotes the same passage in 'Une Mère de glace', *Speculum*, p. 110, with other passages about the 'emptiness' of matter in Plotinus and Plato.

39 C.S. Lewis, *Oxford History of Sixteenth Century Poetry and Prose* (1954), p. 505.

40 See Shakespeare's Sonnets nos 3, 24, 43 and 62.

41 Kingsley Amis, 'A Bookshop Idyll', collected in *The Penguin Book of Contemporary Verse*, ed. Kenneth Allott (1965).

42 Cf. Shakespeare's Sonnets, Marvell's 'To His Coy Mistress', Catullus' 'Vivamus, mea Lesbia'.

43 Edmund Wilson, 'Edna St Vincent Millay', in *The Shores of Light* (1951), p. 747.

44 *Ibid.*, pp. 755–6.

45 Millay, 'I, being born a woman', no. xli of *Collected Sonnets* (1970), p. 41.

46 Jane Stanborough, 'Edna St Vincent Millay and the Language of Vulnerability' *Shakespeare's Sisters*, ed. Gilbert and Gubar, p. 196.

47 *Ibid.*

48 *Ibid.*

49 Edmund Wilson, *op. cit.*, p. 752.

50 Christina Rossetti, preface to 'Monna Innominata', *Poetical Works*, ed. W.M. Rossetti (1904), p. 58.

51 Ellen Moers, *Literary Women*, p. 165.

52 C. Rossetti, *op. cit.*

53 C. Rossetti, from 'The Heart Knoweth Its Own Bitterness' (1857), *Poetical Works*, ed. W.M. Rossetti (1904) p. 152.

54 Lacan, *Le Séminaire XX, 1972–1973, 'Encore'* (1975).

55 Rossetti, 'Monna Innominata' sonnets ii and xiv.

56 Millay, 'Loving you less than life', no. xl in *Collected Sonnets*.

57 T.H. White, journal entry quoted by Sylvia Townsend Warner in *T.H. White: A Biography*, p. 288 (cf n. 18 above).

5 'THE LIPS THAT NEVER LIE'

1 Quotations from 'A still – Volcano – Life', Emily Dickinson, *Complete Poems*, no. 601, and Adrienne Rich, 'Transcendental Etude', *Dream of a Common Language*.

2 Mary Gentile, 'Adrienne Rich and Separatism: The Language of Multiple Realities', *Maenad*, vol. 2, no. 2 (Winter 1982), p. 137.

3 *Ibid.*, p. 142.

4 Adrienne Rich, 'Power and Danger: The Work of a Common Woman', *On Lies, Secrets and Silence*, p. 249.

5 See Irigaray, *Ce Sexe qui n'en est pas un*, especially 'La "Mécanique" des Fluides'.

6 Carolyn Burke, 'Irigaray through the Looking-Glass', *Feminist Studies*, vol. 7, no. 2 (Summer 1981), p. 294.

7 Irigaray interviewed by Lucienne Serrana and Elaine Hoffman Baruch, *Women Writers Talking*, ed. Janet Todd (1983), pp. 238–9.

8 Texts by and about Irigaray before the published translations of *Speculum* and *Ce Sexe* ... include 'When Our Lips Speak Together', tr. Carolyn Burke, *Signs*, vol. 6, no. 1 (1980); 'And the One Doesn't Stir Without the Other', tr. Helène Vivienne Wenzel, *Signs*, vol. 7, no. 1 (1981); and the extracts from the title essay of *Ce Sexe qui n'en est pas un* in *New French Feminisms*, ed. Elaine Marks and Isabelle de Courtivron (1982). There is also an interview with Irigaray in *Ideology and Consciousness*, no. 1 (1977), and another in *Women Writers Talking* (see n. 7 above).

9 See Monique Plaza, 'Phallomorphic Power and the Psychology of "Woman"', tr. Miriam David and Jill Hodges, *Ideology and Consciousness*, no. 4 (Autumn 1978). Parveen Adams associates Irigaray with separatist feminism in 'Representation and Sexuality', *m/f*, no. 1 (1978), p. 77, and Kate McLuskie in the article 'Women's Language and Literature: A Problem in Women's Studies' treats Irigaray as an essentialist (*Feminist Review*, no. 14, Summer 1983, pp. 57–8). For corrective judgments, see Carolyn Burke's article cited above (n. 6); also Mary Jacobus's article 'The Question of Language', *Writing and Sexual Difference*, ed. Elizabeth Abel (1982); also the discussion of Irigaray in Deborah Cameron's *Feminism and Linguistic Theory* (1985).

10 See 'La Tache aveugle d'un vieux rêve de symétrie' ('The Blind Spot of an Old Dream of Symmetry'), *Speculum* (1974), pp. 9–161, *passim*.

11 From 'L'Incontournable Volume' ('The Unshapable Mass'), *Speculum*, pp. 283–4 (my translation).

12 Irigaray interviewed in *Ideology and Consciousness*, no. 1 (1977), p. 75.

13 Irigaray interviewed in *Women Writers Talking*, ed. Todd, pp. 238–9.
14 Adrienne Rich, 'Transcendental Etude', *Dream of a Common Language*.
15 See Adrienne Rich, 'Compulsory Heterosexuality and Lesbian Existence', *Signs*, vol. 5, no. 4 (1980), reprinted by Onlywomen Press as a pamphlet, 1981.
16 W.H. Auden, 'The Question', *Collected Shorter Poems* (1966).
17 *Ibid.*
18 Irigaray, 'And the One Doesn't Stir Without the Other', tr. Hélène Vivienne Wenzel, *Signs*, vol. 7, no. 1 (1981), p. 62.
19 Virginia Woolf, *Mrs. Dalloway* (Penguin, 1974), p. 10.
20 See Mary Jacobus, review of *The Madwoman in the Attic*, *Signs*, vol. 6, no. 3 (Spring 1981), pp. 517–18.
21 Frederick Goldin, *The Mirror of Narcissus* (1964), pp. 98–9.
22 Irigaray, *Speculum*, p. 282 (my translation).
23 See Irigaray, title essay of *Ce Sexe qui n'en est pas un* and 'La Mécanique des fluides' in the same book.
24 Irigaray 'Ce Sexe qui n'en pas un', translated in *New French Feminisms*, ed. Marks and de Courtivron, p. 103; see *Ce Sexe* ... (1977), p. 28.
25 Irigaray, interview in *Ideology and Consciousness*, no. 1, pp. 64–5.
26 See Cora Kaplan's article 'Language and Gender', *Papers on Patriarchy* (1976), for a discussion of the privileged relation between phallus and meaning in language.
27 Emily Dickinson, 'A still – Volcano – Life' (see n. 1 above).
28 See in particular the essay 'La Mécanique des fluides', from *Ce Sexe* ...
29 *Ce Sexe* ..., pp. 116–17.
30 Irigaray, 'When Our Lips Speak Together', tr. Carolyn Burke, *Signs*, 1980, vol. 6, no. 1 (1980), p. 75.
31 Adrienne Rich, 'Twenty-One Love Poems', no. XI, *The Dream of a Common Language*.
32 Cf. the essay 'Pouvoir du discours, subordination du féminin' in *Ce Sexe* ... and Mary Jacobus's discussion of it in 'The Question of Language', in *Writing and Sexual Difference*, ed. Abel.
33 Irigaray, 'Ce Sexe qui n'en est pas un', translated in *New French Feminisms*, ed. Marks and de Courtivron, p. 104; see p. 29 of the original (1977).
34 *Ibid.*, p. 103; see p. 28 of the original (1977).
35 See Monique Plaza, 'Phallomorphic Power', *Ideology and Consciousness*, no. 4 (Autumn 1978): 'Luce Irigaray closes us in the shroud of our own sex, reduces us to the state of child-

women; illogical, mad, prattling, fanciful ... thus is woman' (p. 31).

36 'When Our Lips Speak Together', tr. Burke, *Signs*, vol. 6, no. 1, p. 75.

37 T.S. Eliot, 'The Love Song of J. Alfred Prufrock', *Collected Poems* (1963).

38 Sappho, 'To a Young Girl', no. 141 in the *Oxford Book of Greek Verse* (my translation).

39 Irigaray, 'Quand nos lèvres se parlent', *Ce Sexe qui n'en est pas un*, p. 208 (my translation).

40 Helène Vivienne Wenzel, 'The Text as Body/Politics: An Appreciation of Monique Wittig's Writings in Context', *Feminist Studies*, vol. 7, no. 2 (Summer 1981).

41 Wittig, *The Lesbian Body*, tr. David Le Vray (1976), p. 21.

42 *Ibid.*, preface, p. vii.

43 *Ibid.*, pp. 21, 39 and 32. The 'list of heroines' is enumerated on pp. 67–8.

44 *Ibid.*, p. 17.

45 *Ibid.*, p. 32.

46 Title of article by Alicia Ostriker: 'The Thieves of Language: Women Poets and Revisionist Mythmaking', *Signs*, vol. 8, no. 1 (Spring 1982).

47 For extremity of consciousness, see Wittig, *The Lesbian Body*, pp. 25, 85 and 109; for death-into-life see pp. 17, 92 and 112.

48 Helène Wenzel, *op. cit.*, p. 282 (cf. n. 40 above).

49 Wittig, *The Lesbian Body*, p. 66.

50 *Ibid.*, pp. 109–10.

51 Cf. Chapter 4, p. 101, for suggestion of symmetry between the recognition of sexual difference and the beginning of narrative.

52 Lewis Carroll, *Through the Looking-Glass*, ch. XII, 'Which Dreamed It?'

53 Sylvia Townsend Warner, 'Drawing you, heavy with sleep', *Collected Poems*, ed. Claire Harman (1982).

54 STW's lifelong commitment to Valentine Ackland is no secret; see her *Selected Letters*, ed. and intr. William Maxwell (1983).

55 STW's 'Drawing you, heavy with sleep' is dated by her editor as written in 1935; see *Collected Poems*, p. 276.

56 For an excellent discussion of the representation of female identity in these poems, see Susan Van Dyne's essay 'The Mirrored Vision of Adrienne Rich', *Modern Poetry Studies*, vol. 8 (1977), pp. 141–73.

57 'Women and Honor' was originally read at a workshop in 1975 (see Adrienne Rich, *OLSS*, p. 185). The sequence 'Twenty-One

Love Poems' is dated in *The Dream of a Common Language* as 1974–6 (p. 36).

58 Rich, 'Women and Honor', *OLSS*, pp. 186–7.

59 Linda Anderson 'The Poetry of Adrienne Rich', *Writing/Women*, vol. 1, no. 3 (June 1982), p. 56.

60 Rich, 'Women and Honor', *OLSS*, p. 191, 'The liar fears the void'.

61 *Ibid.*, pp. 191–2.

62 Robert Graves, 'Dialogue on a Headland', *Poems Selected by Himself* (1974).

63 Adrienne Rich interviewed by Elly Bulkin in *Conditions: Two* (1977), p. 58.

64 For a very useful discussion of the significance of women's articulation, see Naomi Scheman's article 'Anger and the Politics of Naming', *Women and Language in Literature and Society*, ed. Sally McConnell-Ginet, Ruth Borker and Nelly Furman (1980).

65 In Greek mythology, Amphritrite is a Nereid, and wife of Poseidon. See the *Oxford Companion to Classical Literature*, ed. P. Harvey (1962), p. 25.

66 See Exodus, ch. XVI, verses 14–21, especially 21: 'They gathered it every morning, every man according to his eating.'

67 Christina Rossetti, 'Monna Innominata', XII.

68 Adrienne Rich, 'Power and Danger', *OLSS*, p. 250.

69 Adrienne Rich, 'Transcendental Etude', *Dream of a Common Language*.

70 'Compulsory Heterosexuality' is the title of Rich's article cited in n. 15 above. For criticism of Rich I have drawn on Cora Kaplan's article 'Wild Nights' in *Formations of Pleasure* (1983), pp. 30–4.

71 Cf. Mary Gentile's article 'Adrienne Rich and Separatism' (see n. 2 above).

72 Wordsworth, *The Prelude* (1852), Book XI, lines 142–4.

SELECT BIBLIOGRAPHY

Place of publication is London unless otherwise stated.

ABEL, Elizabeth (ed.), *Writing and Sexual Difference*, Harvester Press, Brighton, 1982.

AMOS, Valerie, and PARMAR, Pratibha, 'Challenging Imperial Feminism', *Feminist Review*, no. 17 (Autumn 1984).

BAGNOLD, Enid, *A Diary without Dates*, Virago, 1978.

BARTHES, Roland, *The Pleasure of the Text*, Hill & Wang, New York, 1975.

BARTHES, Roland, *Image – Music – Text*, Fontana, 1979.

BARTHES, Roland, *A Lover's Discourse*, Hill & Wang, New York, 1978.

BENJAMIN, Walter, *Illuminations*, Fontana, 1973.

BETTELHEIM, Bruno, *The Uses of Enchantment: The Meaning and Importance of Fairy Tales*, Peregrine, 1978.

BOSTON, Lucy, *Time Is Undone*, Heffers, Cambridge, 1977.

BROUMAS, Olga, *Beginning with O*, Yale University Press, New Haven, Conn., 1977.

BULKIN, Elly, and LARKIN, Joan (eds), *Lesbian Poetry: An Anthology*, Persephone Press, Watertown, Mass., 1981.

BURKE, Carolyn, 'Irigaray through the Looking-Glass', *Feminist Studies*, vol. 7, no. 2 (Summer 1981). (See also under Irigaray.)

CAMERON, Deborah, *Feminism and Linguistic Theory*, Macmillan, 1985.

CHODOROW, Nancy, *The Reproduction of Mothering: Psychoanalysis and the Sociology of Gender*, University of California University Press, Berkeley, 1978.

COWARD, Rosalind, *Patriarchal Precedents*, Routledge & Kegan Paul, 1983.

COWARD, Rosalind, *Female Desire*, Paladin, 1985.

DICKINSON, Emily, *Complete Poems*, ed. Thomas H. Johnson, Faber, 1970.

DINNERSTEIN, Dorothy, *The Mermaid and the Minotaur: Sexual*

Arrangements and Human Malaise, Harper & Row, New York, 1977.

ELLMANN, Mary, *Thinking About Women*, Virago, 1979.

FREUD, Sigmund, *Beyond the Pleasure Principle*, Hogarth Press, 1974.

FREUD, Sigmund, *Case Histories* ii (*Penguin Freud*, vol. 9), 1979.

FUSSELL, Paul, *The Great War and Modern Memory*, Oxford University Press, 1975.

GENTILE, Mary, 'Adrienne Rich and Separatism: The Language of Multiple Realities', *Maenad*, vol. 2, no. 2 (Winter 1982).

GILBERT, Sandra, 'Costumes of the Mind: Transvestism as Metaphor in Modern Literature', in *Writing and Sexual Difference*, ed. E. Abel, 1982.

GILBERT, Sandra, 'Soldier's Heart: Literary Men, Literary Women, and the Great War', *Signs*, vol. 8, no. 3 (Spring 1983).

GILBERT, Sandra, and GUBAR, Susan, *The Madwoman in the Attic: The Woman Writer and the Nineteenth Century Literary Imagination*, Yale University Press, New Haven, Conn., 1979.

GILBERT, Sandra, and GUBAR, Susan (eds), *Shakespeare's Sisters: Feminist Essays on Women Poets*, Indiana University Press, Bloomington, 1979.

GOLDIN, Frederick, *The Mirror of Narcissus*, Cornell University Press, Ithaca, NY, 1964.

GRAHN, Judy (i) Poetry: *The Work of a Common Woman*, St Martin's Press, New York, 1978.

———*Queen of Wands*, The Crossing Press, New York, 1982.

GRAHN, Judy (ii) Prose: *The Highest Apple: Sappho and the Lesbian Poetic Tradition*, Spinsters Ink, San Francisco, 1985.

GRAVES, Robert, *Goodbye to All That* (1929); rev. edn, Cassell, 1957.

GRAVES, Robert, *Poems Selected by Himself*, Penguin, 1974.

HAMPSTEIN, Elizabeth, 'A Woman's Map of Lyric Poetry', *College English*, vol. 34, no. 8 (May 1973).

H.D. (Hilda Doolittle), *Trilogy*, Carcanet Press, Manchester, 1973.

HOMANS, Margaret, *Women Writers and Poetic Identity*, Princeton University Press, Princeton, NJ, 1980.

IRIGARAY, Luce, *Speculum, de l'autre femme*, Editions de Minuit, Paris, 1974.

———*Ce Sexe qui n'en est pas un*, Editions de Minuit, Paris, 1977.

———*Et l'une ne bouge sans l'autre*, Editions de Minuit, Paris, 1979.

IRIGARAY, Luce – In translation: *Speculum of the Other Woman*, Cornell University Press, Ithaca, NY, 1985.

———*This Sex Which is Not One*, Cornell University Press, Ithaca, NY, 1985.

————'When Our Lips Speak Together', tr. Carolyn Burke, *Signs* vol. 6, no. 1 (1980).

————'And the One Doesn't Stir Without the Other', tr. Helène Vivienne Wenzel, *Signs*, vol. 7, no. 1 (1981).

IRIGARAY, Luce – *Interviews: Ideology and Consciousness*, no. 1, 1977.

————*Women Writers Talking*, ed. Janet Todd, 1983.

JACOBUS, Mary (ed.), *Women Writing and Writing About Women*, Croom Helm, 1979.

JACOBUS, Mary, 'The Question of Language', *Writing and Sexual Difference*, ed. E. Abel, 1982.

JARRELL, Randall, *Kipling, Auden & Co.*, Carcanet Press, Manchester, 1981.

JOYCE, James, *A Portrait of the Artist as a Young Man* (1916), rept. Cape, 1964.

JUHASZ, Suzanne, *Naked and Fiery Forms*, Harper & Row, New York, 1976.

KAPLAN, Cora (ed.), *Salt and Bitter and Good: Three Centuries of English and American Women Poets*, Paddington Press, New York, 1975.

KAPLAN, Cora, 'Language and Gender', *Papers on Patriarchy*, PDC and Women's Publishing Collective, Brighton, 1976.

KAPLAN, Cora, *Sea Changes: Essays on Culture and Feminism*, Verso, 1986.

KAPLAN, Cora, 'Wild Nights', in *Formations of Pleasure*, Routledge & Kegan Paul, 1983; collected in *Sea Changes*.

KAZANTZIS, Judith, *The Wicked Queen*, Sidgwick & Jackson, 1980.

KLEIN, Melanie, *Love, Guilt and Reparation*, Hogarth Press, 1975.

————*Narrative of a Child Analysis*, Delta, New York, 1975.

KLEPFISZ, Irena, *Keeper of Accounts*, Persephone Press, Watertown, Mass., 1982.

KRISTEVA, Julia, *Semiotike: Recherches pour une semanalyse*, Tel Quel, Paris, 1969.

LACAN, Jacques, *Ecrits: A Selection*, tr. A Sheridan, Tavistock, 1977.

LAPLANCHE, J., and PONTALIS, J.P., *The Language of Psychoanalysis*, Hogarth Press, 1973.

LOCHHEAD, Liz, *The Grimm Sisters*, Next Editions, 1981.

LOMAX, Marion (ed.), *Time Present and Time Past: Poets at the University of Kent 1965–1985*, Yorick Books, Canterbury, 1985.

LORDE, Audre, *The Black Unicorn*, Norton, New York, 1978.

MANNONI, Maud, *The Child, His 'Illness' and the Others*, Penguin, 1973.

MARKS, Elaine, and DE COURTIVRON, Isabelle (eds), *New French Feminisms: An Anthology*, Harvester Press, Brighton, 1982.

MILLAY, Edna St Vincent, *Collected Sonnets*, Harper & Row, New York, 1970.

MITCHELL, Juliet, *Psychoanalysis and Feminism*, Pelican, 1976. (See also with Jacqueline Rose.)

MOERS, Ellen, *Literary Women*, The Women's Press, 1978.

MOHIN, Lilian, *Cracks*, Onlywomen Press, 1978.

MOHIN, Lilian (ed.), *One Foot on the Mountain: An Anthology of British Feminist Poetry 1969–1979*, Onlywomen Press, 1979.

OLSEN, Tillie, *Silences*, Delta, New York, 1979.

OSTRIKER, Alicia, 'The Thieves of Language: Women Poets and Revisionist Mythmaking', *Signs*, vol. 8, no. 1 (Spring 1982).

PLATH, Sylvia, *Collected Poems*, ed. Ted Hughes, Faber, 1981.

PLAZA, Monique, 'Phallomorphic Power and the Psychology of "Woman"', tr. Miriam David and Jill Hodges, *Ideology and Consciousness*, no. 4 (Autumn 1978).

REILLY, Catherine (ed.), *Scars Upon My Heart: Women's Poetry and Verse of the First World War*, Virago, 1981.

RICH, Adrienne (i) Poetry: *Poems Selected and New, 1950–1974*, Norton, New York, 1975.

———*The Dream of a Common Language*, Norton, New York, 1978.

———*A Wild Patience Has Taken Me This Far*, Norton, New York, 1981.

———*The Fact of a Doorframe*, Norton, New York, 1985.

RICH, Adrienne (ii) Prose: *Of Woman Born*, Virago, 1975.

———*On Lies, Secrets and Silence*, Virago, 1980. (Cited as *OLSS*.)

———*Compulsory Heterosexuality and Lesbian Existence* (from *Signs*, vol. 5, no. 4 (1980), reprinted by Onlywomen Press, London, as a pamphlet, 1981).

RICH, Adrienne: Interview with Elly Bulkin in *Conditions: Two*, 1977.

ROSE, Jacqueline, and MITCHELL, Juliet, *Feminine Sexuality*, Macmillan, 1983.

ROSSETTI, Christina, *Poetical Works*, with memoir and notes by W.M. Rossetti, Macmillan, 1904.

SEXTON, Anne, *Transformations*, Oxford University Press, 1972.

SMITH, Stevie, *Collected Poems*, Allen Lane, 1975.

SMITH, Stevie, *Selected Writing*, ed. Hermione Lee, Faber, 1983.

STEVENSON, Anne (i) Poetry: *Correspondences*, 1974.

———*Minute by Glass Minute*, Oxford University Press, 1982.

STEVENSON, Anne (ii) Prose: 'Writing as a Woman', in *Women Writing and Writing about Women*, ed. Mary Jacobus, Croom Helm, 1979.

———'The Poetry of Carol Rumens', *PN Review* no. 46 (vol. 12, no. 2), 1985.

TODD, Janet (ed.), *Gender and Literary Voice*, Holmes & Meier, 1981.

TODD, Janet, *Women Writers Talking*, Holmes & Meier, 1983.

WARNER, Sylvia Townsend, *Collected Poems*, ed. Claire Harman, Carcanet Press, Manchester, 1982.

WARNER, Sylvia Townsend, *T.H. White: A Biography*, Chatto & Windus, 1967.

WENZEL, Helène Vivienne, 'The Text as Body/Politics: An Appreciation of Monique Wittig's Writings in Context', *Feminist Studies*, vol. 7, no. 2 (Summer 1981). (See also under Irigaray.)

WILSON, Edmund, *The Shores of Light*, W.H. Allen, 1952.

WIMSATT, W.K., *The Verbal Icon*, University Press of Kentucky, Lexington, 1954.

WINNICOTT, D.W., *Playing and Reality*, Penguin, 1980.

WITTIG, Monique, *The Lesbian Body*, tr. David Le Vray, Avon Books, New York, 1976.

WORDSWORTH, Willam, *Lyrical Ballads*, ed. Derek Roper, Oxford University Press, 1964.

YALE FRENCH STUDIES, no. 62, *Feminist Readings: French Texts/ American Contexts*, New Haven, Conn., 1981.

INDEX